60 YEARS OF *Fender* ®

SIX DECADES OF THE GREATEST ELECTRIC GUITARS TONY BACON

60 YEARS OF FENDER

SIX DECADES OF THE GREATEST ELECTRIC GUITARS

by TONY BACON

A BACKBEAT BOOK
Second edition 2010
First edition (as *50 Years of Fender*) 2000
Published by Backbeat Books
An Imprint of Hal Leonard Corporation
7777 West Bluemound Road,
Milwaukee, WI 53213
www.backbeatbooks.com

Devised and produced for Backbeat Books by
Outline Press Ltd
2A Union Court, 20-22 Union Road,
London SW4 6JP, England
www.jawbonepress.com

ISBN: 978-0-87930-966-4

DESIGN: Paul Cooper Design
EDITOR: Siobhan Pascoe
PHOTOGRAPHY: Miki Slingsby

Origination and print by Regent Publishing Services Limited, China

10 11 12 13 14   5 4 3 2 1

CONTENTS

"Fender's first decade
was one of brilliant
design, the foundation
upon which much
of the company's
subsequent success
has been built."

50s

Broadcasting begins

Fender's electric lap-steel guitars and amplifiers (highlighted in this 1950 catalog, right) enjoyed limited local success, and Leo Fender considered a solidbody electric guitar. This became the Esquire, then the Broadcaster, and then the Telecaster. One of the first players to embrace the new Fender was ace West Coast sessionman Jimmy Bryant (above), but it wasn't long before guitarists everywhere would crave Fender electric guitars.

Leo Fender was not entirely alone in his desire to create a solidbody electric guitar. But, crucially, his would be the first commercially available.

Electric guitars had been around since the 1930s, at first mainly steel guitars for playing on the lap, but soon joined by regular hollowbody guitars with crude, early pickups screwed on.

Rickenbacker in California was the first with a pickup employing the electro-magnetic principle since used on virtually every electric guitar, and Gibson set the style for the best hollowbody electrics, offering models such as the fine ES-175 of 1949.

Some musicians and guitar-makers had been wondering about the possibility of a solidbody instrument. It would be without the annoying feedback often produced by amplified hollowbodies, and allow louder playing. It would also be cheaper to produce. Rickenbacker had launched a semi-solid Bakelite-body electric guitar in the mid 1930s. Around 1940 in New Jersey guitarist Les Paul built a test-bed electric with a solid central block of pine. And in 1948 in Downey, California – just 15 miles or so from Leo Fender's base – Paul Bigsby made a solidbody through-neck guitar for country artist Merle Travis.

Leo Fender's new solidbody was the instrument that we know now as the Fender Telecaster, effectively the world's first commercially successful solidbody electric guitar. As we shall see in this book, the design is still very much alive today. The guitar was originally named the Fender Esquire and then the Fender Broadcaster, and it first went into production in 1950.

It was a simple, effective instrument. It had a basic, single-cutaway, solid slab of ash for a body, with a screwed-on maple neck. Everything was geared to easy production. It had a slanted pickup mounted into a steel bridge-plate carrying three adjustable bridge-saddles, and the body was finished in a yellowish color known as blond. It was unadorned and like nothing else. It was ahead of its time.

Production of the instrument began at Fender's two small steel buildings on Pomona Avenue in Fullerton, Los Angeles, during the first half of 1950. By November, despite serious cash-flow problems, the guitar had a truss-rod and two pickups, and a new name: the Fender Broadcaster.

It did not prove immediately easy to sell. Prototypes taken to a music show were laughed at and disparagingly called canoe paddles or snow shovels. A salesman trying to sell one in San Francisco was offered in exchange the electric train-set of a potential customer's son. It was not an auspicious start for the solidbody electric guitar. However, time would reveal the Fender Broadcaster as one of the most historically significant musical instruments ever made.

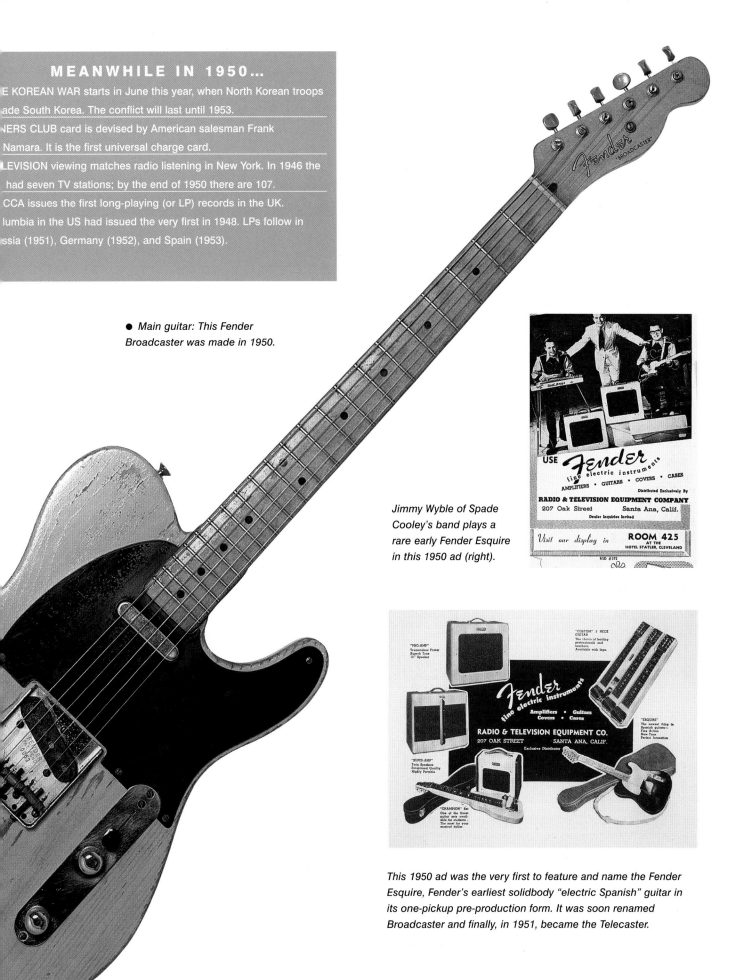

● *Main guitar: This Fender
Broadcaster was made in 1950.*

*Jimmy Wyble of Spade
Cooley's band plays a
rare early Fender Esquire
in this 1950 ad (right).*

*This 1950 ad was the very first to feature and name the Fender
Esquire, Fender's earliest solidbody "electric Spanish" guitar in
its one-pickup pre-production form. It was soon renamed
Broadcaster and finally, in 1951, became the Telecaster.*

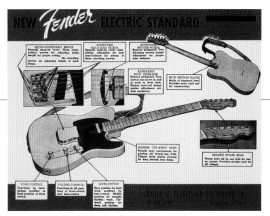

When Fender introduced a solidbody electric bass guitar at the end of 1951, no one knew what to make of the strange new hybrid. It looked like a long-necked version of the Telecaster, but it had four strings, tuned an octave below the lower four strings of a guitar. It was another remarkable innovation from Fender: the world's first commercially-made electric bass guitar. In time it would completely transform the sound of popular music.

Fender started to produce the Fender Precision Bass in October 1951. It shared much of its construction with the Broadcaster, which during 1951 had been renamed the Telecaster. Gretsch, a large New York-based instrument manufacturer, indicated its prior use of "Broadkaster" on various drum products. At first, Fender simply used up its Fender Broadcaster decals on the guitar's headstock by cutting off "Broadcaster," leaving the Fender logo. These instruments are known among collectors today as Nocasters.

The new name decided upon for the two-pickup Fender solidbody was Telecaster (1953 example, far left) while a new single-pickup version re-used the earlier Esquire name (1953 Esquire, near left). Meanwhile, the new Precision Bass was going into production with a 20-fret maple neck bolted to a pale yellow "blond" ash body. There was a black pickguard and finger-rest, a single-coil pickup, a chromed metal plate under a volume and tone control, and a chromed cover each for the bridge and for the pickup. The bridge had two saddles that carried two strings each, and the strings passed from there through the body, anchored at four fixing points on the rear.

The Precision was typical of Fender's early products. It had an austere simplicity and was geared to easy, piece-together construction. The tuning of the Fender bass, E-A-D-G, was the same as the double-bass, an octave below the lower four strings of the guitar. This familiarity was designed to attract guitarists looking for a new instrumental skill, as well as double-bass players seeking portability. The electric bass guitar had arrived... though no one took much notice.

The Precision's body design was new for Fender, with an extra cutaway that broke away from the single-cutaway Telecaster and would later inspire the body shape of Fender's Stratocaster guitar. The extra cutaway was needed because the bass's longer neck and heavier tuners would have made a Telecaster-shape design unbalanced. However, by extending the top horn and relocating the strap peg, the balance was effectively restored.

In those years at the start of the 1950s few other guitar companies took seriously Fender's new direction with the electric bass. Forrest White, Fender's production chief from 1954, once said that people who weren't sure if Leo was crazy when he brought out the solidbody guitar were quite certain when they saw the electric bass.

● *Main guitar: This Precision
Bass was among the first to
leave the factory in 1951.*

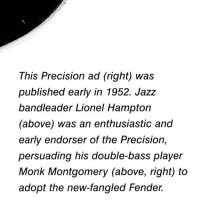

*This Precision ad (right) was
published early in 1952. Jazz
bandleader Lionel Hampton
(above) was an enthusiastic and
early endorser of the Precision,
persuading his double-bass player
Monk Montgomery (above, right) to
adopt the new-fangled Fender.*

Fender
Precision
Bass . . . . AMAZINGLY
DIFFERENT

FRETTED NECK
SUPERB TONE
EASILY PLAYED
MODERN DESIGN
HIGHLY PORTABLE
EXTREMELY RUGGED
FASTER CHANGES
A NEW PLAYING
SENSATION

LIGHT WEIGHT
1/6 SIZE REGULAR BASS
NOW IN USE BY
MANY OF AMERICA'S
LEADING ARTISTS

BASSMAN AMPLIFIER

● Especially designed for bass reproduction
● Custom designed Jensen; 15" Jensen speaker
● True fidelity bass reproduction
● Excellent volume characteristic
● Rugged construction

DISTRIBUTED EXCLUSIVELY BY

RADIO & TELEVISION EQUIPMENT CO.

207 OAK STREET   SANTA ANA. CALIF.

Studying the steel

Despite the exciting new developments in solidbody guitars and basses, in the early 1950s Fender's main business was in electric steel guitars and amplifiers. The 1952 ad (above) illustrates this well, showing the early-style "TV" amp cabinets. Later in the year Fender introduced one of its most famous models, the Twin Amp (later catalog, right), which inaugurated a new "wide panel" cabinet style.

Since Leo Fender's days in the mid 1940s running the shortlived K&F company with Doc Kauffman, small instrument-amplifiers and electric steel guitars had been mainstays of his business. These products continued to be vitally important to the new Fender company, and the lines were rapidly expanded.

The steel had been the first type of guitar to go electric in the 1930s, and had become popularized as an easy-to-play instrument suitable for beginners. The electric steel had also gained enormous appeal among professional musicians, especially in Hawaiian music, as well as in country and western bands. The steel guitar was played on the lap or mounted on legs. The name came not from its construction – Fender's steels were all wooden – but from the metal bar used in the player's left hand to stop the raised strings, which were generally tuned to an open chord.

Fender's single-neck steels available before 1950 had included the Organ Button (the odd name derived from its switchable muted "organ"-tone effect), the cheap Princeton with hardwired cord, the long-lived Deluxe which survived in various guises until 1980, and the Champion model. The latter was renamed as the Student in 1952 as a come-on to the booming teaching "studios" of the time. An example of the Student model is pictured opposite.

It was natural for Fender to adapt some of the features of his existing steel guitar designs for the new solidbody instruments. Clearly the Fender Telecaster and Precision Bass had borrowed stylistic elements from the steel's pickup and cover and the control knobs and plate. In fact, one of the early prototypes for the Esquire/Broadcaster even had the steel's more pointed headstock with three tuners each side, but this was quickly changed to the better known design with six tuners in a line.

Amplifiers too had developed quickly. The pre-1950 Fender line included early wooden-handled Model 26 versions of the Deluxe, Professional and Princeton, as well as an angled-front twin-speaker model, the Dual Professional (soon renamed Super), and a remodeled series in "TV-front" cabinets using the soon famous tweed-pattern cloth covering.

In 1951 along came the Bassman amp, intended to amplify the new Precision Bass but today highly regarded by guitar players. The following year saw another new item, the Twin Amp, this one aimed from the outset at guitarists. It became the top model in Fender's amplifier line, boasting 15 watts output through twin 12-inch speakers, and all in a new-design "wide panel" cabinet. The grille in this type (see Deluxe, opposite) is squared off and extended further out than the old "TV" style, with wide panels above and below. The whole amplifier line – including Bandmaster, Bassman, Deluxe, Princeton, Pro Amp and Super – was restyled to reflect the new look.

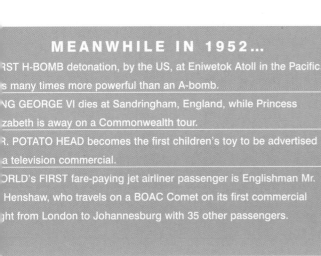

MEANWHILE IN 1952...

RST H-BOMB detonation, by the US, at Eniwetok Atoll in the Pacific. s many times more powerful than an A-bomb.

NG GEORGE VI dies at Sandringham, England, while Princess zabeth is away on a Commonwealth tour.

R. POTATO HEAD becomes the first children's toy to be advertised a television commercial.

ORLD's FIRST fare-paying jet airliner passenger is Englishman Mr. Henshaw, who travels on a BOAC Comet on its first commercial ght from London to Johannesburg with 35 other passengers.

● *Main guitar: This Student steel model was made in about 1954.*

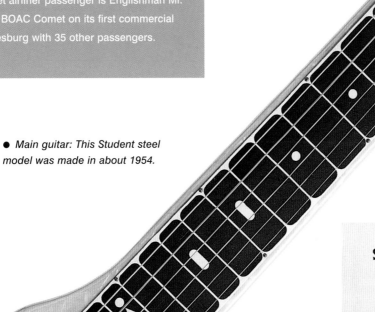

The Student steel was sold in a budget-price set with a matching amplifier (below).

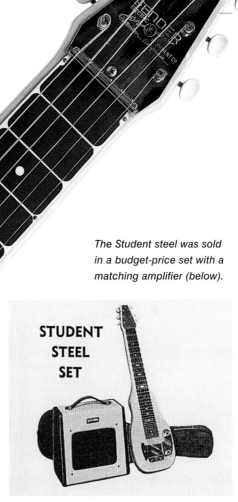

STUDENT STEEL SET

This little Deluxe amp (right) was made with the new "wide panel" cabinet design and covered in "tweed" cloth. The Twin Amp featured in the catalog opposite (top of page) is in the later "narrow panel" style.

Sales & Swing

Fender made multi-neck steel guitars from the earliest days: the two-neck Dual 8 Professional, for example, was launched in 1946, and the triple-neck Custom followed three years later. Multi-neck steel guitars provided players with the means to change quickly between tunings, although the pedal-steel guitar would dispose of this rather unwieldy arrangement. Many of the western swing steel players of the 1950s drew their driving electric guitar runs from Fender models such as the Stringmaster.

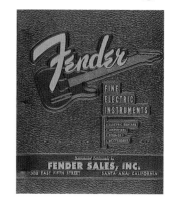

At first, Fender products were distributed by the Radio & Television Equipment Company ("Radio-Tel") which was based in Santa Ana, some 15 miles south of Fullerton. Don Randall was general manager of Radio-Tel, which was owned by Francis Hall.

But early in 1953 the set-up was re-organized into a new Fender Sales distribution company, operational by June. Based like Radio-Tel in Santa Ana, Fender Sales had four business partners: Leo, Don Randall, Francis Hall, and Charlie Hayes.

Hayes, who had been Radio-Tel's first salesman, was killed in a road accident in 1955, while in late 1953 Hall bought the Rickenbacker company. So in 1955 Fender Sales would become a partnership between Leo and Don Randall, though it was Randall who actually ran this pivotal part of the Fender business.

In 1953 Fender had three new buildings put up on a three-and-a-half acre plot at South Raymond Avenue and Valencia Drive in Fullerton. Clearly expansion of Fender's product lines was imminent.

As well as just two electric guitars, the Telecaster and Esquire, Fender had at this time a line of seven amplifiers (Bandmaster, Bassman, Champ, Deluxe, Princeton, Super, Twin Amp), five electric steel guitars in various versions (Custom, Deluxe, Dual, Stringmaster, Student) and its revolutionary electric bass guitar, the Precision.

But clearly the company wanted to make more models. *The Music Trades* magazine reported in 1953 that with the new property Fender hoped that production would be upped by almost 100 per cent in the next few months. A significant new project begun in 1953 would turn into Fender's best known instrument, the Stratocaster. An important addition to the Fender team occurred in 1953 with steel guitarist Freddie Tavares, principally to help Leo design new products. Freddie and Leo worked together developing plans for the new solidbody Strat. But for the time being it was western swing that was bringing the electric guitar to popularity in the United States. Western swing was a lively dance music that had grown up in Texas dancehalls during the 1930s and 1940s.

Many of western swing's steel-guitar players used Fender electrics, notably Noel Boggs with Spade Cooley and Leon McAuliffe with Bob Wills. But there were also some "Spanish" guitarists in the ranks, such as Telecaster-wielding Bill Carson with Hank Thompson's Brazos Valley Boys. However, Fender's days of reliance on its steel guitar lines was soon to end. Business began to pick up for the company as news of the solidbody "Spanish" Telecaster and Esquire spread among guitarists, and as the new Fender Sales got into gear and its salesmen – soon growing to Art Bates, Mike Cole, Dave Driver, Charlie Hayes, and Don Patton – began to persuade more instrument-store owners to stock Fenders.

The Stringmaster below may
have belonged to Leon McAuliffe
(above), the great steel-guitar
player who joined Bob Wills's
Texas Playboys at age 18.

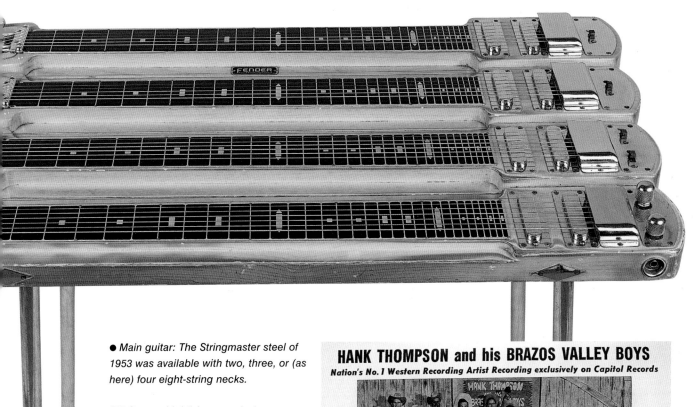

● Main guitar: The Stringmaster steel of
1953 was available with two, three, or (as
here) four eight-string necks.

Bill Carson (right) is seen playing a
Telecaster in Hank Thompson's band, an
outfit that played a commercial fusion of
western swing and honky tonk. The band
had a big hit with 'The Wild Side Of Life'
in 1952 (this line-up is from a year later).

Strataclysmic

Leo Fender listened hard to players' comments about the Telecaster and Esquire models, and during the early 1950s he and Freddie Tavares began to devise the guitar that would become the Stratocaster (seen in stylized form on the 1954 catalog cover, right). At first other makers had merely mocked Fender's new solidbody guitars, but soon Gibson had joined in with its Les Paul, Gretsch with the Duo Jet, Kay with its K-125. Competition was looming – and Fender needed to up the stakes. This they most certainly did.

The Stratocaster was launched during 1954. Samples around May and June were followed by the first proper production run in October. The new Fender guitar was the first solidbody electric with three pickups, meaning a range of fresh tones, and featured a new-design vibrato unit that provided pitch-bending and shimmering chordal effects.

The new vibrato – often called a "tremolo" by Fender and many others since – was troublesome in development. But the result was the first self-contained vibrato unit: an adjustable bridge, a tailpiece, and a vibrato system, all in one. It wasn't a simple mechanism for the time, but a reasonably effective one. It followed the Fender principle of taking an existing product (in this case, the Bigsby vibrato) and improving it. Fender's new vibrato had six bridge-pieces, one for each string, adjustable for height and length, which meant that the feel of the strings could be personalized and the guitar made more in tune with itself. The complete unit was typical of Fender's constant consideration of musicians' requirements and his application of a mass-producer's solution.

The Strat came with a radically sleek, solid body, based on the outline of the 1951 Fender Precision Bass. Some musicians had complained to Fender that the sharp edge on the Telecaster's body was uncomfortable – the dissenters included musician/entertainer Rex Gallion and Western Swing guitarist Bill Carson – and so the Strat's body was contoured for the player's comfort. Also, it was finished in a yellow-to-black sunburst finish.

Even the output-jack mounting was new, recessed in a stylish plate on the body face. And the headstock? Side by side with Paul Bigsby's guitar made for Merle Travis in 1948 there is clearly influence from the earlier instrument. But as a whole the Fender Stratocaster looked like no other guitar around, especially the flowing, sensual curves of that beautifully proportioned, timeless body.

The Stratocaster's new-style pickguard complemented the lines perfectly, and the overall impression was of a guitar where all the components ideally suited one another. The Fender Stratocaster has since become the most popular, the most copied, the most desired, and very probably the most played solid electric guitar ever. On its 40th anniversary in 1994 an official estimate put Strat sales at over a million guitars. At its launch it wasn't such a world-beater; later in the 1950s, the Fender Stratocaster began to hint at future glories, especially in the hands of players such as Buddy Guy, Carl Perkins, and Buddy Holly.

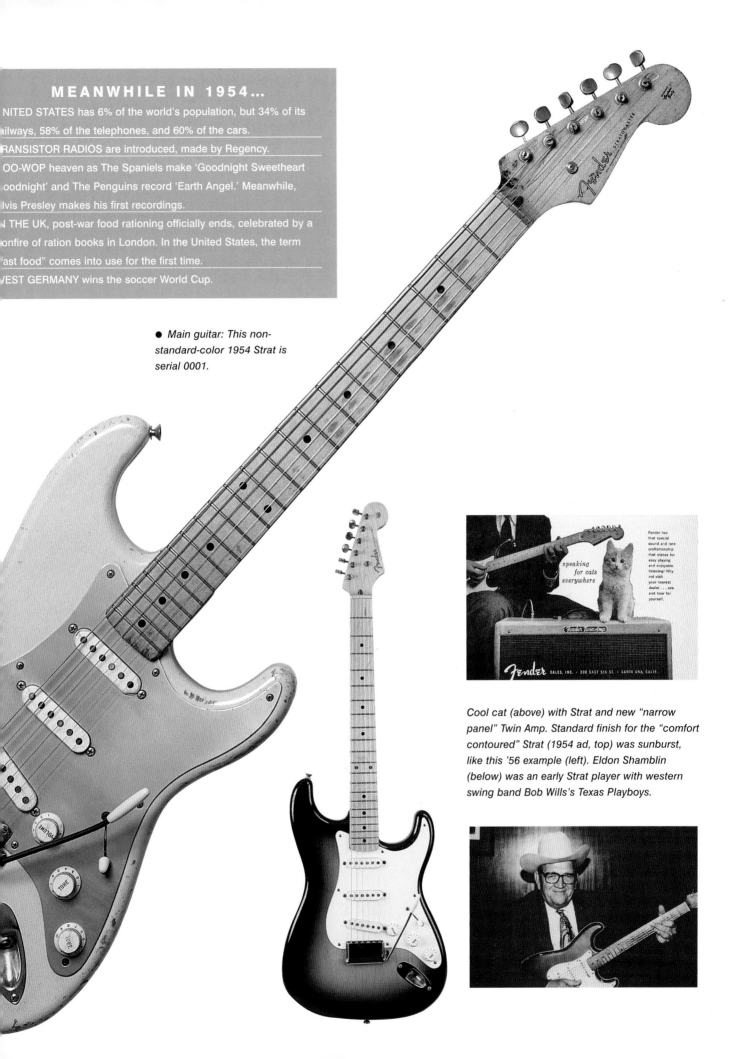

● *Main guitar: This non-standard-color 1954 Strat is serial 0001.*

speaking for cats everywhere

Fender has that special sound and rare craftsmanship that makes for easy playing and enjoyable listening! Why not visit your nearest dealer . . . see and hear for yourself.

Fender SALES, INC. • 308 EAST 5th ST. • SANTA ANA, CALIF.

Cool cat (above) with Strat and new "narrow panel" Twin Amp. Standard finish for the "comfort contoured" Strat (1954 ad, top) was sunburst, like this '56 example (left). Eldon Shamblin (below) was an early Strat player with western swing band Bob Wills's Texas Playboys.

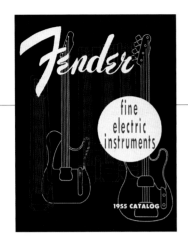

Switched-on Tremolo

Fender's new Strat did not have an immediate impact, and only later in rock'n'roll did it find its true home. For the time being, Fender continued to advertise its established lines – including the Telecaster and Precision Bass, pictured on the covers of the two 1955 catalogs shown here (above and right). Steel guitars appeared virtually unchanged, but Fender continued to innovate in its ever-popular line of amplifiers.

Forrest White was a new and important addition to the Fender ranks at this time. He was in effect the head of production, and gradually organized the somewhat haphazard working methods into a more efficient and effective operation. White had already met Leo a few times when, in spring 1954, the two had lunch and Leo asked Forrest if he'd be interested in helping to sort out a number of what he described as "management problems" at Fender. Leo knew that the operation was close to collapse. Sometimes Fender checks would bounce locally: Leo had no credit and often had to pay cash for materials. White's timing was perfect, and he joined the company.

Forrest White helped to turn things around, along with Don Randall who was busy bolstering sales, and Freddie Tavares who was Leo's main ideas man in the design of new amplifiers and guitars.

Guitarist Bill Carson was still among the musicians whose views were sought by the Fullerton-based Fender team when designing the new products that any manufacturer must continually produce. Carson would often take out prototype amplifiers for testing and evaluating at local gigs, leaving the unit with other players for a while so that he could monitor a range of opinions to feed back to the factory. Leo would sometimes appear at the gigs, walk right up to the amp, mid-song, and – oblivious to the musicians – begin to fiddle with settings. Carson has said that none of the musicians particularly relished these visits from

Leo and many of them simply considered him "a pest."

One of the new amplifier effects being developed was what Fender called "tremolo," a regular, rhythmic fluctuation in volume, previously heard on home organs. The model that introduced the effect to the Fender amplifier line was the Tremolux, a 15-watt amp with single 12-inch speaker. It was launched in 1955. One of the tubes in the Tremolux's circuit was used as an oscillator in order to provide the distinctive tremolo sound, which could be switched on and off as required by the player. But this reallocation of tube duty did limit the power output of the amp. As the circuitry improved, tremolo would become a popular amplifier effect, not least in the work of players such as Link Wray and Duane Eddy.

Fender's amplifiers in 1955 ranged from the top-of-the-line 50-watt Twin Amp, now in classic "narrow panel" style and with two 12-inch speakers, priced at $279.50, down to the 4-watt Champ (sometimes called Student) with 6-inch speaker at just $59.50.

At the bottom of the steel guitar pricelist sat the humble Student (the renamed Champion model), but this was replaced in 1955 by the Champ, a more straightforward design with straight body sides, retaining the single slanted Telecaster-style pickup and simple volume-and-tone controls.

● *Main guitar: This Champ steel
guitar was made around 1958.
The model was also sold as a set
(ad, bottom of page), with a
matching amp, for around $120.*

*The Tremolux (above) was the first Fender amplifier to feature the
new "tremolo" effect, best described as a rhythmic fluctuation in
volume. Steel guitarist Pete Drake (modest LP jacket, below)
would go on to play with Bob Dylan, including the sessions for
the classic Nashville Skyline album.*

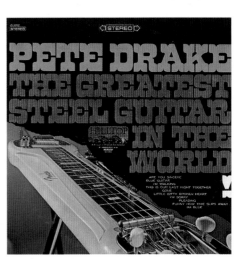

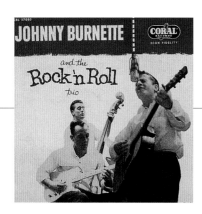

Schoolroom guitars

Just as rock'n'roll began to rise in the US, Fender shifted its electric guitar line downward. The company launched two new low-end electrics, the Duo-Sonic and the Musicmaster, specifically to cater for the army of beginners enlisted by music stores keen for a new customer base. A solidbody electric Mandolin was also new In the company's catalog (top), while ads (right) continued to stress Fender's existing lines, including steels, amps, and the new solidbody guitars.

A common marketing method to increase sales of guitars and many other musical instruments during the 1950s was the "school" or "studio," usually run at musical instrument stores after-hours and offering lessons to would-be players. Naturally such a school was well situated to sell a start-up instrument to the beginner... and equally attentive when the new musician felt his or her skills demanded a better and more expensive instrument with which to show off this new-found talent.

Fender was as aware of these marketing tactics as any go-ahead American instrument manufacturer and sales outfit of the time. So it was that the company introduced in 1956 a pair of new "student" electrics. These two new instruments – the Duo-Sonic and the Musicmaster -– had a shorter 22½-inch scale-length as opposed to Fender's customary 25-inch scale. The "three-quarter size" one-pickup Musicmaster and two-pickup Duo-Sonic were described in the company's ads and catalogs as being "ideal for students and adults with small hands."

They were clearly designed for players on a tight budget, for those starting out on electric guitar who flocked to the retailers' schools. The two new guitars certainly looked cheaper than Fender's Stratocaster, Telecaster, and Esquire – and indeed they sat at the bottom of Fender's pricelist. Around this time the Strat with vibrato listed at $274.50, the Tele at $199.50, Esquire at $164.50, Duo-Sonic at $149.50, and the

Musicmaster at $119.50. One apparently attractive feature of the Duo-Sonic and Musicmaster (and a few early Stratocasters) was what Fender called "gold-finished pickguards." These 'guards were in fact made from a gold-colored anodized aluminum. The metal provided excellent electrical shielding, meaning less extraneous noise. However, the anodized-like "skin" soon wore through to the aluminum below as the player strummed and picked, leaving unsightly gray patches. The anodized 'guards did not last much beyond the 1950s.

Rock'n'roll burst on to the scene in 1956, and players such as Carl Perkins at Sun Records and Paul Burlison in The Rock'n'Roll Trio (jacket, top) seized on the bright, cutting sound of Fender's solidbody electrics.

Aside from rock'n'roll, Fender looked back to a traditional instrument for its other new model for 1956: the electric Fender Mandolin. It sold for $169.50, with a Fender-style double-cutaway solid body and four strings rather than the regular mandolin's eight (in four pairs). Perhaps surprisingly, the Mandolin lasted in the line until the mid 1970s.

● *Main guitar: This blond Duo-Sonic with anodized 'guard was made in 1959.*

Most Fenders came with point-of-sale material such as this instruction booklet (below right). Fender described the Duo-Sonic and Musicmaster (ad, below left) as three-quarter size. The neck (and scale) was shorter than other Fenders.

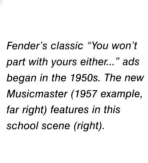

Fender's classic "You won't part with yours either..." ads began in the 1950s. The new Musicmaster (1957 example, far right) features in this school scene (right).

Low-note heaven

It was becoming clear that rock'n'roll was not only going to change popular music for good, but that it would also have a fundamental effect upon the fortunes of the Fender company. Buddy Holly's 1957 debut album *The Chirping Crickets* (above) visibly declared to a growing band of fans his preference for the Fender Stratocaster. And in studios and stages across America the newly configured Fender Precision bass was beginning to provide a new, solid foundation for a brand new music.

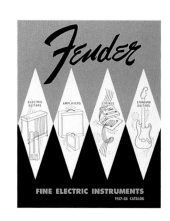

Some makers had joined in after Fender had marketed the first electric bass guitar in 1951 – Kay in 1952, Gibson in 1953, Danelectro in 1956 – but popular use of the electric bass guitar still remained scarce. The emerging rock'n'roll music at first stayed in the hands of double-bass players: Marshall Lytle with Bill Haley's Comets, Joe B. Maudlin with Buddy Holly's Crickets, and Bill Black with Elvis Presley.

However, Black got a Fender Precision in early 1957: he certainly had one in the MGM studios during the filming of *Jailhouse Rock*, and Presley's title track recorded in April sounds like Black is using his new Fender. This stamp of approval was important for Fender's basses, and many fellow players noted Black's adoption of the new-fangled electric bass guitar.

By 1957, Fender basses were being seen more frequently on stage. Contemporary photos reveal a Precision in the live bands of Jerry Lee Lewis and B.B. King, among others. Looking back now, it seems remarkable that the electric bass took so long to become established. Fender had made some minor changes to the design of the Precision in 1954, contouring the body and painting it in two-tone sunburst like the Strat. But in 1957 some more fundamental changes were made. Most important was a brand new split-coil pickup with a more defined and solid bass sound. Fender also redesigned the shape and bulk of the instrument's headstock, enlarging it to help overall balance as well as to improve resonance and the

uniformity of individual notes. It was unusual for Fender to make such major changes to an existing production model, and it seems to have indicated that the company was still searching for a combination of features that would appeal to and attract the new breed of electric bassists.

A more minor change was the new-shape Precision pickguard, which at first was of the anodized aluminum type. These final alterations of 1957 – the new pickup, larger headstock, and different pickguard – defined the look of the Precision for decades to come.

Fender also announced early in 1957 a Strat in see-through blond finish and gold-plated hardware. This was later called the "Mary Kaye" thanks to musician Kaye appearing with one in a number of Fender catalogs of the period (an example can be seen at the top of the page). This Strat with its gold hardware and blond finish was Fender's first official Custom Color guitar – although the term has since been more popularly applied to guitars finished in solid colors. As we shall see, Fender would eventually come up with a defined list of Custom Colors.

● *Main guitar: This Precision
Bass was made during 1957.*

*Donald "Duck" Dunn (above, right),
played a Precision Bass in the
1960s with Booker T & The MGs.
Speedy West is pictured (jacket,
right) playing a Fender 1000 steel.
This 1957 Strat (above) is a "Mary
Kaye" version, with gold hardware
and blond finish. Don Randall (far
right) is pictured about to pilot
Fender's Piper aircraft in 1957.*

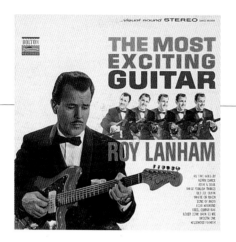

Jazzy circuitry

With Musicmaster and Duo-Sonic established at the bottom of the pricelist, Fender now tried to expand the higher end of its list, and the company introduced the all-new Jazzmaster model during 1958. Never the most popular Fender, the Jazzmaster did at least offer the first glimpse of a Fender rosewood fingerboard, a feature that was soon adopted for other models. Altogether more unusual was the Fender Electric Violin that also debuted in 1958.

For its next model introduction Fender created a distinctly high-end instrument. The Jazzmaster first appeared in Fender sales material during 1958, and at some $50 more than the Strat it became the new top-of-the-line model. Fender could not resist tagging the new Jazzmaster as "America's finest electric guitar... unequalled in performance and design features."

Immediately striking to the electric guitarist of 1958 was the Jazzmaster's unusual offset-waist body shape, which became the subject of one of Fender's now growing number of patents. For the first time on a Fender, the Jazzmaster featured a separate rosewood fingerboard glued to the customary maple neck, aimed to give a more conventional appearance. The Jazzmaster's floating vibrato system was new, too, and had a tricky "lock-off" facility aimed at preventing tuning problems if a string should break.

The controls were certainly elaborate for the time, and at first were set in one of Fender's "gold" anodized-like pickguards. A small slide-switch selected between two individual circuits, offering player-preset rhythm and lead sounds. The idea was a good one: the ability to set up a rhythm sound and a lead sound, and switch between them. But the system seemed over-complicated to players brought up on straightforward volume and tone controls.

The sound of the Jazzmaster was richer and warmer than players were used to from Fender. The name Jazzmaster had not been chosen at random, for Fender was aiming this different tone at jazz players, who at the time largely preferred hollowbody electrics, and principally those by Gibson.

However, jazz guitarists found little appeal in this new, rather difficult solidbody guitar – and mainstream Fender players largely stayed with their Stratocasters and Telecasters.

The Jazzmaster certainly marked a change for Fender, and constituted a real effort to extend the scope and appeal of the company's guitar line. Ironically, and despite some early successes, this has been partly responsible for the Jazzmaster's lack of long-term popularity relative to the Strat and Tele, mainly as a result of players' dissatisfaction with the guitar's sounds and playability. A limited resurgence of interest came with punk in the 1970s and, later, grunge.

After the electric solidbody Mandolin, Fender could not resist trying its electric approach with another traditional instrument – the violin. The Fender Electric Violin debuted in 1958, with a solid maple body, special pickup, and typical Fender-style controls and jack. The Fender-shape headstock was routed with a single slot to reveal the tuner spindles. Despite high hopes for this "advancement in amplified violin qualities" Fender withdrew the Violin after less than a year. However, it did reappear in slightly modified form in the late 1960s for a rather longer run.

● *Main guitar: This Jazzmaster was made in 1959.*

The Jazzmaster figured strongly in Fender's continuing "You won't part with yours either..." ad series.

Fender continued to make a series of "hang-tags" (two for the Jazzmaster, below) to help store owners entice customers.

Custom bound

Reacting to criticism that its guitars were plain, Fender introduced the new bound-edge sunburst Telecaster Custom and Esquire Custom. Custom Color Fenders were also appearing more often, and the 1958/59 catalog was Fender's first with a color cover (above), a Fiesta Red Strat prominently displayed. The company was still keen to experiment, even with publicity, and came up with this unusual ad (right) showing an X-rayed amplifier.

During all the changes and additions to the Fender line in its first decade, the humble Telecaster – in effect Fender's first solidbody electric guitar – had stayed almost exactly the same. Cosmetic alterations included a change from the original black to a white pickguard at the end of 1954 (like the example in the 1959 ad, below). Otherwise the Telecaster was largely the same blond-finished guitar it had been in 1951. Some 1950s Telecasters had been made in non-standard colors, and a few small batches had been finished in sunburst. In 1959, however, two new models joined the Fender line that gave a quite different look when compared to the continuing regular Telecaster and the single-pickup Esquire. These were the Telecaster Custom and the Esquire Custom. Each had a sunburst-finish body with bound edges. Binding is a technique that creates a thin white strip on the edge between the top and sides and back and sides of the guitar, and was more often seen on hollowbody guitars such as those made by Gibson.

The new Customs also had rosewood fingerboards, as on the Jazzmaster. During 1959 the new separate rosewood fingerboard on a maple neck was adopted for all the other existing Fender models – regular Telecaster and Esquire, Stratocaster, Duo-Sonic, and Musicmaster. It replaced Fender's previous construction that laid frets directly into the face of a solid maple neck.

Guitarists in Britain had been unable officially to buy any US-made guitars since 1951 when a ban on imports had been imposed. However, enterprising singer Cliff Richard had approached the Fender factory in California in 1959 after his guitarist, Hank Marvin, had pointed out the strange concoction known as a Fender Stratocaster pictured on a Buddy Holly record sleeve. Marvin was soon the owner of one of the first Stratocaster in the UK, and his group The Shadows displayed it to thousands of adoring fans as Cliff and the group began their rise to fame. During 1959 the import ban was lifted, and US guitars could once again be legally sold in Britain.

A new amplifier, the Vibrasonic, introduced some fresh features to the Fender line in 1959. It had a new style of cabinet with a sloping, front-mounted control panel, and was finished in a hard-wearing vinyl material, Tolex, that replaced Fender's classic "tweed" linen covering.

An early Strat in the UK (red guitar, below) was bought by Cliff Richard for Shadows man Hank Marvin (pictured below with a later Strat).

● Main guitar: This Telecaster Custom was made in 1963.

Fender's flyer (below left) illustrates the Tele Custom, standing, and the Esquire Custom, lying beside it. The cheery scene on the 1959/60 catalog cover (below right) has the American family at home, with mom clutching the headstock of a Telecaster Custom, alongside Strat, Jazz Bass, and Duo-Sonic.

"As rock music exploded with electric guitars at the core, Fender provided perfectly malleable tools for the new sonic revolutionaries."

60s

Now color me Jazz

Fender's fine new electric bass guitar was the Jazz Bass model. It brought a new level of luxury to the Fender bassist and produced a wider tone, largely a result of its new pair of eight-pole "strip" pickups. Bright news for Fender's Custom Color fans was a newly prepared chart that illustrated samples of all the available color options, while over in Britain the new Fender distributor published its first advertisement (right).

The new Fender Jazz Bass began to appear from the factory in March 1960. Having established with the ground-breaking Precision that the bass guitar was an important new instrument with a unique voice that would help to define pop music, the next step for Fender was to make an upscale model.

The design of the Jazz Bass was distinguished by its offset-waist body, similar in style to the Jazzmaster guitar launched two years earlier. The Jazz Bass also differed from the Precision in its narrow string spacing at the nut, which gave the neck a distinctly tapered feel, and its provision of two pickups which offered wider tonal possibilities. For many years the Precision Bass outsold the more expensive Jazz Bass: some preferred the out-and-out simplicity of the P-Bass; others opted for the crisper tones and different feel of the Jazz.

The pickups of the Jazz Bass were connected in humbucking mode, as was the "split" pickup used on the Precision since 1957. Leo Fender later explained to several interviewers that in the 1950s Fender never emphasized the humbucking capabilities of these pickups because the company's patent attorney had told them that such pickups had been patented back in the 1930s. Leo explained that humbuckers were introduced on the basses because he thought the earlier single-coil pickup was too hard on the amp's loudspeakers, whereas the humbucking types offered a softer, less spiky signal – no doubt easing the Fender amp-repair department's workload.

Pop groups began to emerge in the early 1960s with all-guitar line-ups (plus drums), a significant change that would benefit Fender enormously. In the US one of the leading instrumental bands was The Ventures. They later moved to a business relationship with Mosrite guitars, but for the first few years they played Fenders, as gloriously displayed on early jackets (above left). In the UK the top instro group was The Shadows. They are seen with singer Cliff Richard in the first UK ad for Fender guitars (above), placed in 1960 by Fender's new British distributor Jennings (who also marketed Vox amps).

Fender's Custom Colors reached an important new level in 1960 when the company issued its first color chart, showing all the options available. Fender used paints by Du Pont, which was a supplier to America's big car factories. Fender opted for Du Pont's Duco nitro-cellulose lines, such as Fiesta Red or Foam Green, as well as the more color-retentive Lucite acrylics, with names like Lake Placid Blue Metallic or Burgundy Mist Metallic.

● *Main guitar: This Teal Green Jazz Bass dates from 1964.*

Bobby seen (below) in the basement, mixing up the Jazz Bass. An unlikely sight, maybe, but Fender issued this ad around 1967. At first the Jazz Bass had two "stacked" control knobs, as on these early artful Fender catalogs (above). Meanwhile, newly popular instrumental groups like The Ventures (jacket, opposite page) loved Fenders.

At first the Jazz Bass had two "stacked" control knobs, as on this early flyer (above). Later versions had three controls.

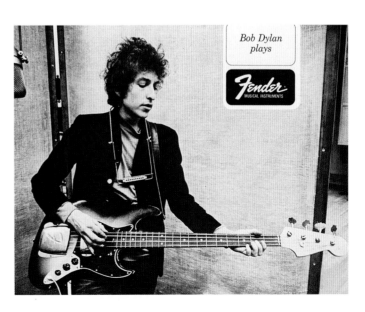

Between a regular guitar and a bass dwelt the six-string bass, introduced to the Fender line as the VI model in 1961. This year also saw the rise of surf music, personified by Dick Dale (the left-hander with the Strat, top). Years later, Dale's distinctive Strat (on the sleeve, left) would prompt a signature model from the modern Fender operation. Back in 1961, Fender amplifiers split into "piggyback" form with the new Showman.

The New Jersey-based Danelectro company had produced the first six-string electric bass guitar in 1956. Guitarists were the target for this new instrument – effectively an electric guitar tuned an octave lower – and the different sound of the Dan'o appealed to players like Duane Eddy as well as to some studio musicians. Other makers noted the popularity, and Fender launched its take on the idea with the VI in 1961. The scheme was to offer an instrument to guitarists who wanted a bass sound: the VI was a guitar with a longer neck, its strings tuned an octave lower than a regular guitar.

Fender's VI (often referred to as the Bass VI) was a specialist instrument, and as such never proved especially popular. Probably its best-known user was British bassist Jack Bruce, who briefly used one in his early Cream days in the 1960s. Some VIs still turn up today in studios for a particular sound, but the tight string-spacing makes them of limited appeal to bass players used to today's instruments.

Fender still understood the value of visual appeal to grab attention at the trade shows it now regularly attended, and after the X-ray amplifier ad of the previous year built a Duo-Sonic with a transparent plastic body for exhibition at the annual NAMM (National Association of Music Merchants) show. A number of other similar see-through Fenders were produced around this time. Meanwhile, guitar-based pop groups were multiplying at a rate that must have

been tremendously satisfying to Fender Sales, with instrumental bands becoming particularly popular. Dick Dale headed one faction when he became known as the "king of the surf guitar." Left-hander Dale (Dick and band, with his distinctive Strat, are pictured at the top of the page) poured out surging, staccato lines, borrowing scales from an East European heritage, all set adrift in a sea of reverb. His big hit was 1961's 'Let's Go Trippin',' but surf music didn't last much beyond the British invasion of 1964.

In the amplifier department at Fender a new kind of set-up was introduced with the "piggyback" Showman rig. This had the electronics housed in a separate box that sat on top of the separate speaker cabinet: a familiar arrangement now, but new at the time. Also new to the 1961 Fender line was reverberation (or "reverb"), created with a vibrating spring. The effect had been developed by the Hammond organ company for use on its home instruments. At Fender, it first appeared in the separate Fender Reverb unit, but a few years later made its way into amps such as the Vibroverb as a switchable effect.

● *Main guitar: This VI was made
in 1962 – still with the original
three-switch panel on the body.*

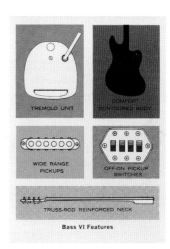

*This later 1960s catalog
(above) details various VI
features, including the
guitar's newer four-switch
control panel.*

*Some amps, including the
Showman (top), changed to
Fender's new "piggyback"
two-piece style in 1961. A
later 1960s catalog (left)
reveals a VI (second from
right) with features such as a
four-switch panel and block-
shape fingerboard markers.*

1962
A spin in the Jag

Not content with the relatively expensive Jazzmaster, Fender introduced a new top-of-the-line model in 1962: the Jaguar. Like the earlier Jazzmaster, it was another offset-waist multi-control instrument, and the Jag seemed an attractive proposition, but still it failed to dent the supremacy of Fender's dynamic duo, the Tele and the Strat. Steve Cropper (above) of Booker T & The MGs showed just how effective the noble Tele could be in the right surroundings.

The next new guitar to leave Fender's production line was the Jaguar, which first showed up in sales material during 1962. The Jag used a similar offset-waist body shape to the earlier Jazzmaster, and also shared that guitar's separate bridge and vibrato unit, although the Jaguar had the addition of a spring-loaded string mute at the bridge. Fender rather optimistically believed that players would prefer a mechanical string mute to the natural edge-of-the-hand method. They did not. There were some notable differences between the Jaguar and Jazzmaster. Visually, the Jag had distinctive chromed control panels, and was the first Fender with 22 frets. Its 24-inch scale-length ("faster, more comfortable") was shorter than the Fender standard of 25 inches and closer to that of Gibson. It gave the Jag a different playing feel compared to other Fenders. The Jaguar had better pickups than the Jazzmaster. They looked much like Strat units but had metal shielding added at the base and sides, no doubt as a response to the criticisms of the Jazzmaster's tendency to noisiness. The Jag's electrics were yet more complex than the Jazzmaster's, using the same rhythm circuit but adding a trio of lead-circuit switches.

Like the Jazzmaster, the Jaguar enjoyed a burst of popularity when introduced. But this new top-of-the-line guitar, "one of the finest solid body electric guitars that has ever been offered to the public" in Fender's original sales hype, never enjoyed sustained success, and has always been marked down as an also-ran.

The Jaguar was offered from the start in four different neck widths, one a size narrower and two wider than normal (coded A, B, C or D, from narrowest to widest, with "normal" B the most common). These neck options were also offered from 1962 on the Jazzmaster and Strat.

In the studio, cool-hand Steve Cropper (pictured at top left of this page) translated the good old Telecaster's simplicity of design into musical terms as his lean guitar lines graced 1962's Booker T & the MGs hit, 'Green Onions.'

From around 1960 in its print advertising Fender had begun to use a modernized "chunky" Fender logo that had been drawn up by Bob Perine, the man responsible for the stylish look of Fender's advertising from the late 1950s to the late 1960s. The Jaguar was the first standard electric guitar to carry the new logo on its headstock. During the following years Fender gradually applied it to all models. In this incarnation (early to mid 1960s) it has become known among collectors as the "transition" logo because it leads from the original thin "spaghetti" Fender logo to a bolder black version introduced at the end of the 1960s.

● *Main guitar: This Jaguar in Candy
Apple Red was made in 1964.*

*Carl Wilson of The Beach Boys
(right) was a prominent player
of the Jaguar in the 1960s, but
the model has never matched
the Stratocaster and Telecaster
for classic Fender playability
and style. Which may explain
why fellow Boy Al Jardine
clutches a Strat. The Jag ads
(below) came out during the
1960s and include the crucial
gigging-by-motorcycle test.*

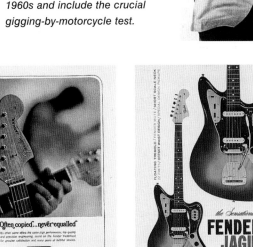

Fenders with air inside

Fender became so excited about the prospect of making its own acoustic guitars that it poached a guitar-maker from fellow California company Rickenbacker and created a brand new factory in which to build the new models. Unfortunately, that enthusiasm did not translate into guitars that matched Fender's great solidbody electrics. This year also saw the introduction of the first Fender–Rhodes electric pianos.

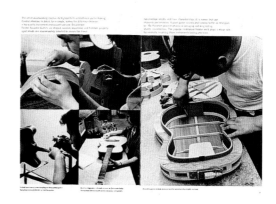

Like most guitar firms operating in the United States in the 1960s, Fender naturally intended to expand its market share. It was simply not considered enough for Fender to be at the forefront of solidbody electric guitar production. But some players felt that the company had taken a step too far when its first acoustic flat-top guitars were announced during 1963.

Fender had marketed flat-top acoustics before. In 1959 the Harmony company of Chicago first supplied Regal-brand equipment for exclusive distribution by Fender, including flat-top acoustics and the R-270 archtop electric. Evidently this arrangement did not prove successful, and the Regal lines were dropped in the early 1960s. Roger Rossmeisl was brought into the company by Leo Fender to design the company's own new flat-top acoustic guitars and to oversee their construction. The acoustics were manufactured at a new plant on Missile Way in Fullerton, about a mile from the main Fender factory.

Rossmeisl was the son of a respected German guitar-maker, Wenzel Rossmeisl, and had come to the United States in the 1950s. At first he had worked for Gibson in Michigan, but soon moved west to Rickenbacker in California. There Rossmeisl's skills became more evident, and he made a number of one-off custom guitars as well as designing production models for Rickenbacker's distinctive Capri and Combo series. Rossmeisl's work also influenced other makers, notably Mosrite of California.

For the Fender acoustics, Rossmeisl gave the instruments the outward look of conventional flat-tops, but for most of them he retained the heel-less bolt-on neck that had served Fender so well for its solidbody electrics. Thus the necks had an "electric" feel, as opposed to the wider necks of most flat-tops.

Rossmeisl also began to fit many of the Fender acoustics with an aluminum support rod inside the body, designed for maximum rigidity. A patent for this "acoustic tension tube" was granted in 1968. Fenders with the tension-tube feature, visible through the guitar's soundhole, are sometimes called "broomstick" models.

The first steel-string acoustic models were the King (later renamed Kingman) and Concert, launched in 1964. There were also steel-string Folk and nylon-string Classic models that had conventional acoustic-guitar construction. The King had the Martin company's much-emulated "dreadnought" wide-shouldered body. Later additions to the flat-top series included the Shenandoah and Villager 12-strings, as well as the Malibu, Newporter, Palamino, and Redondo models. None of these would prove especially popular, but some of these first acoustics stayed in the Fender line until the early 1970s.

● *Main guitar: This Palomino, in
Mahogany finish, was made by
Fender around 1970.*

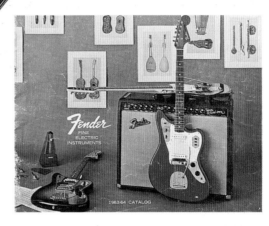

*The colorful 1963/64
catalog cover (above)
features the new
"blackface" Twin Reverb
amp (right).*

*Rick Nelson (left) and
Johnny Cash (below) pose
with one of the new Fender
flat-top acoustic guitars.*

Mustang savvy

As Fender tinkered with its low-end models and Custom Colors, elsewhere musical revolutions were taking place. The Beatles had begun their moves to world domination, branching out spectacularly from local British stardom. And the trend in the UK for young white groups to play black R&B saw 'Little Red Rooster' by Howlin' Wolf (album jacket, right) provide a perfect blueprint for The Rolling Stones.

Fender added a new model this year at the lower end of its pricelist. The Mustang was in effect the $159.50 Duo-Sonic with a vibrato added – for which Fender put on an extra $30 over the price of the Duo-Sonic. The Mustang shared the generally low-end features of the earlier Duo-Sonic, as well as its two single-coil pickups.

At first, the Mustang also shared the "slab" body of the Duo-Sonic – unrefined, squared-off edges without much thought of the player's comfort. But over the next few years Fender gradually introduced a contoured body to all of its "student" models: one-pickup Musicmaster, two-pickup Duo-Sonic, and vibrato-equipped Mustang.

While the existing Duo-Sonic and Musicmaster had previously been available only with a short scale of 22½ inches, from 1964 these models too were made available in optional medium-scale 24-inch versions. The medium-scale models were now known as the Musicmaster II and the Duo-Sonic II. Other minor changes were adopted for the two existing budget models in order to make them more stylistically similar to the new Mustang.

The Mustang was also offered in two different scale-lengths, although short-scale Mustangs were rarely ordered and few were built.

The optional Custom Colors scheme for many models was now well underway, and a new color chart had been issued in 1963. Available colors were Black, Burgundy Mist Metallic, Candy Apple Red Metallic,

Dakota Red, Daphne Blue, Fiesta Red, Foam Green, Inca Silver Metallic, Lake Placid Blue Metallic, Olympic White, Sherwood Green Metallic, Shoreline Gold Metallic, Sonic Blue, and Surf Green. Fender used paints from Du Pont's Duco nitro-cellulose and Lucite acrylic lines which had been developed primarily for use by automobile manufacturers. The names that Fender gave to its Custom Colors came from the original car makers' terms. Fiesta Red, for example, was first used by Ford in 1956 for a Thunderbird color, while Lake Placid Blue originally appeared on a 1958 Cadillac Brougham. When Gibson had copied Fender's idea of Custom Colors for its Firebird series, one of the finishes – a coppery gold – was identical to a Fender shade. Gibson adopted its Oldsmobile name, Golden Mist, because Fender already used the Pontiac term, Shoreline Gold.

Decades later the guitars bearing these original Fiesta Reds, Sonic Blues, and Burgundy Mists, especially from the late 1950s and the 1960s, have proved very collectable. A Custom Color Fender, especially an early one, is rated a prime catch. And this despite the prevalence of "refinishes," so good they can fool many an alleged expert.

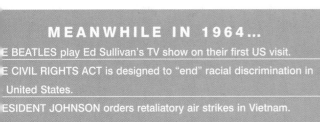

● *Main guitar: This Mustang was
made around 1972.*

*The catalog page (below) shows how the
Duo-Sonic (center) was slightly altered in
1964 to match the new Mustang (far left).*

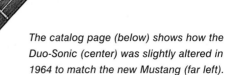

*Two desirable Custom Color guitars are
pictured here (below): a 1963 Jazzmaster,
finished in Foam Green (top); and a 1961
"spaghetti"-logo Stratocaster in Burgundy
Mist (below). Similar models in 1964
would have appeared on Fender's
pricelist intended to sell at $366.97 for
the Jazzmaster and $303.97 for the Strat.*

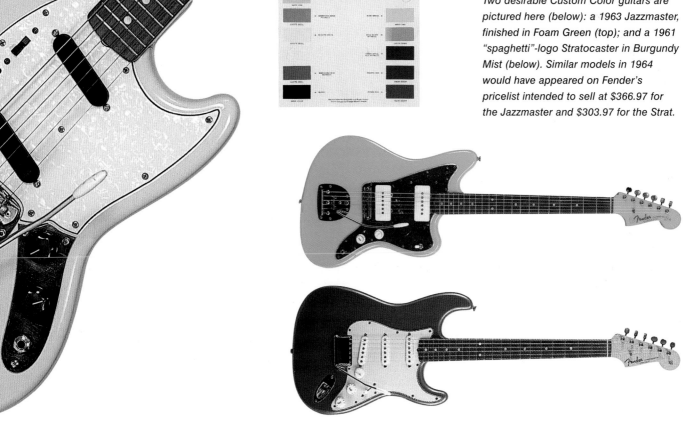

Fender FINE ELECTRIC INSTRUMENTS / 1965-66 CATALOG

1965
Suddenly it's CBS

Fender was sold to CBS at the very start of this year, and for some of the company's fans things would never be the same again. At first the prospects seemed good as the new owner pumped money and enthusiasm into the impressive purchase. But in years to come the relationship would be soured. None of this stopped Fender introducing new models, although the new instruments released for 1965 – the Bass V and the Electric XII – proved shortlived.

Since the launch of the humble Broadcaster in 1950, Fender had turned into an extremely successful company. The rock'n'roll revolution saw the company churning out good, relatively affordable guitars available in large numbers. Fender had captured a significant portion of the new market. Many buildings had been added to cope with increased manufacturing demands, and by 1964 the operation employed some 600 people (500 in manufacturing) spread over 29 buildings. As well as electric guitars, Fender's pricelists offered amplifiers, steel guitars, electric basses, acoustic guitars, electric pianos, effects units, and a host of related accessories.

Sales boss Don Randall remembers writing a million dollars' worth of sales during his first year in the 1950s, which rose to some $10 million in the mid 1960s (translating to something like $40 million of retail sales). Electric guitars were at their peak of popularity, and Fender was among the biggest and most successful producers, selling its products in the US and well beyond. Players as diverse as surf king Dick Dale, bluesman Muddy Waters and pop stylist Hank Marvin – plus thousands of others around and between them – were rarely seen without a Fender in their hands. However, Leo Fender was by all accounts a hypochondriac, and his acute health worries (as well as uncertainties about financing expansion) prompted him to sell Fender. Don Randall handled the sale.

In January 1965, Fender was sold to the mighty Columbia Broadcasting System Inc – better known as CBS. The purchase price was a staggering $13 million, by far the highest ever paid in the musical instrument industry for a single manufacturer. In fact, it was about $2 million more than CBS had recently paid for the New York Yankees baseball team. CBS executive Goddard Lieberson was bullish about Fender, and announced: "This is a fast growing business tied into the expanding leisure time market. We expect this industry to grow by 23 per cent in the next two years." CBS went on to buy other instrument companies such as Rogers (drums), Steinway (pianos) and Leslie (organ loudspeakers).

While the shock of the change set in – and the sale was to have far-reaching consequences – the Electric XII and Bass V were launched. The V (far left) was an unusual, shortlived 15-fret five-string bass, with a high C-string. Electric 12-strings had recently been popularized by The Beatles and Byrds, both with Rickenbackers. Fender's version was belated. An innovation was the 12-saddle bridge for precise adjustments of individual string heights and intonation. But the 12-string craze of the 1960s was almost over and the Electric XII also proved shortlived, lasting in the line only until 1969.

● *Main guitar: This Electric XII, finished in Candy Apple Red, was made in 1966.*

The 1965/66 catalog (below) had early prototypes of the ill-fated Marauder, with its "invisible" pickups (under the pickguard). Further protos like the one pictured (above) had multiple switches and angled frets, but neither type made it into production.

At this 1969 catalog session (above) Electric XIIs bookend a trio of Teles, while the Fender ad team take another surrealistic wallow (above).

The Coronado guitars and basses, intended as competition for arch-rivals Gibson, were launched by Fender in 1966. They proved once again that Fender ought to stick with solidbody instruments, and none was successful. A cheaper bass model, the Mustang Bass, was also added to the line. Pop music was becoming ever more adventurous, and players like Jeff Beck (right) in The Yardbirds and Robbie Robertson with the newly-electric Bob Dylan were confirmed Fender fans.

PLAYER OF THE MONTH

The Coronado thinline guitars were yet more creations from Roger Rossmeisl's Missile Way acoustic factory and the first electric hollowbody designs to appear from Fender. Clearly, the company was being pushed by new owners CBS to compete with the successful 300-series thinline electrics marketed by the other big name in the guitar market, Gibson.

The Coronados looked like conventional competitors for the Gibson models, with equal-double-cutaway bound bodies that sported large, stylized f-holes. But in fact, just like the earlier flat-tops, they employed the standard Fender bolt-on necks, as well as the company's distinctive headstock design. Options included a new vibrato tailpiece, and there was a 12-string version that used the Electric XII's large curved headstock design. Unfamiliar with some edge-binding techniques, factory hands had to re-do some of the work. To cover up burn marks caused by re-binding, the team devised a special white-to-brown shaded finish – Antigua – to salvage the scorched Coronados. Antigua-finish Coronados would go on sale over the next few years.

In 1967 Fender introduced even more unusual colored versions of the Coronados, the Wildwoods. As pop culture became absorbed with the dazzling, drug-influenced art of psychedelia, Fender predictably announced the Coronado Wildwoods as "truly a happening in sight and sound" with "exciting rainbow hues of greens, blues and golds."

They certainly did look different. The Wildwood effect was achieved by injecting dyes into beech trees during growth, producing in the cut wood a unique colored pattern which followed the grain. Despite all the fuss, the feedback-prone Coronados never caught on, and the various versions would be dropped from the catalog by 1971.

Fender's first short-scale four-string, the Mustang Bass, did little to expand or enhance Fender's line beyond the company's leading bass duo. The type shown (opposite) is the later so-called Competition version, distinguished by contrasting colored stripes on the body.

Over in England, Jeff Beck had struck an early blow for the coming pre-CBS cult – the deification of guitars made before the CBS takeover in 1965 – when he bought a 1954 Esquire and began using it with The Yardbirds. The picture (top right of this page) shows the Esquire before he switched the white pickguard for a "correct" black to move a notch higher in one-upmanship among other vintage-conscious guitarists on the scene. Beck played it on 1966's 'Shapes Of Things' 45 among a jukeboxful of others.

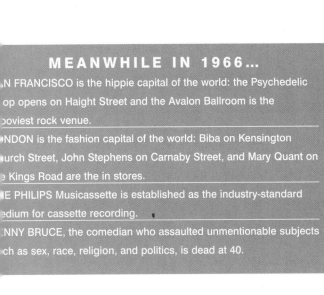

MEANWHILE IN 1966...

N FRANCISCO is the hippie capital of the world: the Psychedelic
op opens on Haight Street and the Avalon Ballroom is the
ooviest rock venue.

NDON is the fashion capital of the world: Biba on Kensington
urch Street, John Stephens on Carnaby Street, and Mary Quant on
e Kings Road are the in stores.

E PHILIPS Musicassette is established as the industry-standard
dium for cassette recording.

NNY BRUCE, the comedian who assaulted unmentionable subjects
ch as sex, race, religion, and politics, is dead at 40.

● *Main guitar: This Wildwood*
Coronado XII, in dye-injected
finish, was made in 1968.

WILDWOOD COLORS *(Color and grain*
varies slightly with each instrument.)

| Wildwood I | Wildwood II | Wildwood III |
| Rainbow Greens | Rainbow Blues | Rainbow Golds |

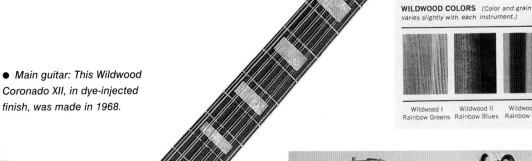

The Byrds (right) pop into Fender for
their Wildwood Coronados – Chris
Hillman on bass (left) and Roger
McGuinn on guitar – but secretly
plan to use only the amps. The
catalog (above) features Coronados
in Wildwood (far left and right) and
Antigua (second left) plus Wildwood
color samples (top).

The new Mustang Bass appeared this
year, and a few years later was offered in
Competition form with a striped body
finish, like the one shown here.

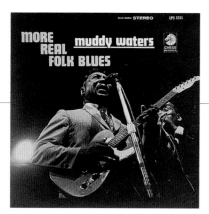

Solid state?... illogical

Catastrophe hit Fender this year as the first examples of its new line of Solid State amps went on sale – and very soon many of them came back as unworkable. It was one of the first signs that CBS might not be acting in the best interests of the many musicians who relied on Fender products. Over in England, meanwhile, Beatles guitarist George Harrison harmonized psychedelia and rockabilly as he set about painting and decorating his "Rocky" Strat (pictured opposite).

Fender launched another of its "student" solidbody electrics this year, the $149.50 Bronco with single pickup and simple vibrato, along with a matching amp. The new guitar was the cheapest in the line, other than the Musicmaster, and lasted in the catalog until the early 1980s. In this lowly area of its pricelist Fender seemed reasonably assured, though elsewhere, as we've seen, uncertainty was creeping in. But amplifiers had always been a safe and reliable part of the company's business. There was of course much more competition now compared to Fender's earliest days, but players generally liked Fender amps – and even if they didn't choose the brand, they admired and respected it.

However, with the new Solid State line, first sold in 1967, Fender made its first big amplification mistake. Internal arguments developed over the project, and in the turmoil Forrest White – who had joined Leo in 1954 – resigned.

Solid state electronics, driven by transistors rather than the conventional tubes, were new and, it seemed at the time, the way to go. Various other makers were introducing solid state amps, and Fender decided it had to join in, despite the squabbling.

Problems were legion as the first models – Solid State Deluxe Reverb, Solid State Pro Reverb, Solid State Super Reverb, and Solid State Vibrolux Reverb – came off the line in 1967. The factory struggled with unfamiliar electronics work, and the repair department was piled with returns. The ultra-clean

sound of the amps that did work was at odds with the kind of distortion-laden music that players such as Jimi Hendrix were popularizing at the time. To many, this part of Fender's line seemed dangerously out of touch. The Solid State amps were dropped by 1970. Fender's strengths were, thankfully, more than enough to rise above such a disaster.

One of the few top bands apparently absent from Fender usage was The Beatles, who in their concert days had contented themselves with an on-stage mix of primarily Epiphone, Gibson, Gretsch, Hofner, and Rickenbacker guitars. Now that they were strictly a studio outfit, other brands had crept into the arsenal, including Fender. George Harrison and John Lennon each acquired a Strat in 1965 for studio use – heard to stinging effect on cuts of the period such as 'Nowhere Man' – and Paul McCartney bought an Esquire around 1967 for six-string recordings. Also this year, Harrison painted his existing Strat with a wild "Rocky" decoration (see opposite), in time for appearances in the band's *Magical Mystery Tour* TV movie. It could hardly go unnoticed.

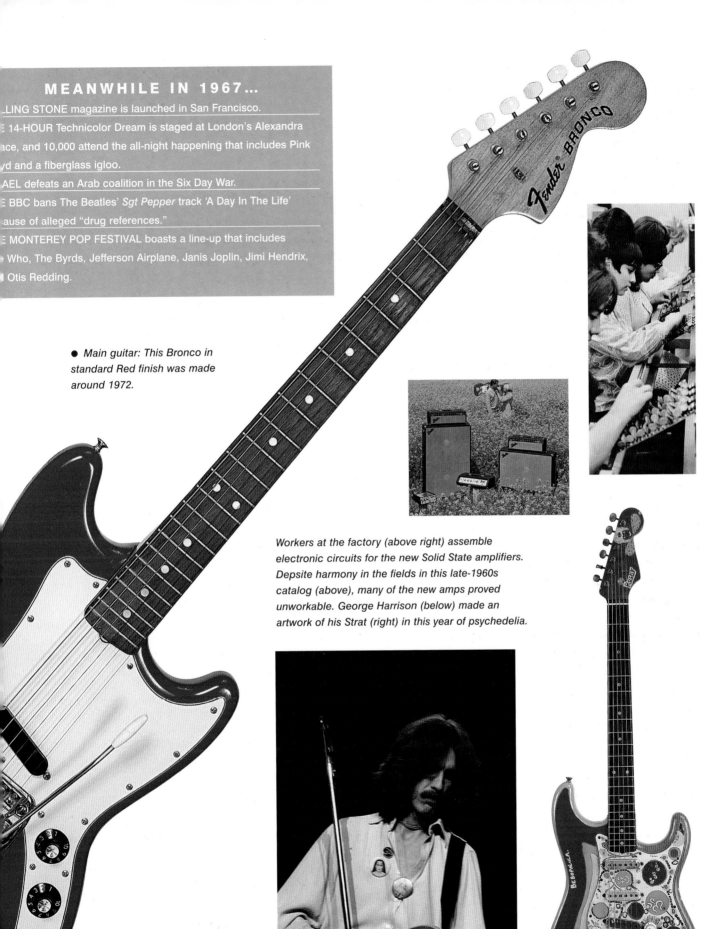

● *Main guitar: This Bronco in standard Red finish was made around 1972.*

Workers at the factory (above right) assemble electronic circuits for the new Solid State amplifiers. Depsite harmony in the fields in this late-1960s catalog (above), many of the new amps proved unworkable. George Harrison (below) made an artwork of his Strat (right) in this year of psychedelia.

PsychoTelec...

As psychedelia arrived at Fender in the shape of the Blue Flower and Pink Paisley Telecaster models, original blues guitarists such as Buddy Guy (right) were helping to inspire an enduring craze in the United States and Europe for blues-rock. Fender's product catalogs continued to develop through the creative eye of adman Bob Perine, as demonstrated on the cover of the company's impressive 1968 brochure (above).

The Telecaster had become a dependable instrument for players in many different kinds of music, but in country the Tele had become almost a membership badge. Musicians admired the guitar and put it into regular service in the country capital in Nashville and also on the West Coast, drawing upon its simplicity that encouraged the voice and character of the individual player to shine out.

During the late 1960s Fender tried a number of variations on the Telecaster. For example, in 1968 psychedelia hit Fender when self-adhesive wallpaper with a paisley or floral pattern was applied to some Telecasters, presumably in order to give them fresh flower-power appeal.

Certainly the Paisley Red and Blue Flower Teles and Tele Basses could not be described as examples of CBS's boring approach to guitar design. But the Tele seemed the least likely target for the creation of such far-out psychedelic art objects. Since its inception in the early 1950s, the model had rarely been seen without its standard blond finish, even though Custom Colors were offered. However, the dazzling wallpaper experiment did not last long. While the company did not immediately seem to grasp the fact, it would nonetheless gradually dawn on Fender that a central part of the Telecaster's lasting appeal is its strong resistance to change.

Another unusual pair of guitars made a first appearance in 1968. Roger Rossmeisl had been let loose with a couple of guitar designs that were even less like the normal run of Fenders than the earlier Coronado models. Rossmeisl's specialty was the so-called "German carve" taught to him by his father, Wenzel. It gives a distinctive indented "lip" around the top edge of the body, following its outline. Rossmeisl adopted this feature for the new hollowbody archtop electric Montego and LTD models (both pctured opposite). Both were eminently traditional, yet again obstinately using Fender's customary bolt-on neck.

From all reports there were very few Montegos and LTDs made, and it has been suggested that some of those which did manage to reach music stores may subsequently have been recalled to the factory because of constructional problems. Rossmeisl had an alcohol problem and did not last much longer at Fender. He died back home in Germany in 1979 at the age of 52.

Some amplifiers began to display a small cosmetic change this year, adopting a new aluminum control panel. These are now known among collectors as "silverface" models to distinguish the color of their control panels from the "blackface" style that preceded them.

● *Main guitar: This Paisley
Red Telecaster was made
around 1968.*

FENDER'S **Blue Flower**

Blue Flower bursts forth in a dazzling array of subtle purple and
green patterns. Never before has such an exciting profusion of
color been offered.   Telecaster $279.50, Telecaster Bass $289.50.
(These finishes are available on the Telecaster and Telecaster Bass only.)

*Roger Rossmeisl designed several
new electric hollowbody guitars
launched in 1968, including the
Montego II (above right) and the LTD
(above left). Fender's psychedelic
Tele and Tele Bass also came in
Blue Flower (right). The steely Tele
of Clarence White featured on The
Byrds' country-flavored album
Sweetheart Of The Rodeo (top).*

Custom clunker

The Woodstock festival marked the end of the 60s. Half a million music lovers were cast in a sea of mud, entertained by musical luminaries such as Jimi Hendrix (left), ablaze with musical passion and communicating through his white Fender Stratocaster. "Musicians want to pull away after a while," he said, "or they get lost in the whirlpool." A year later he was dead at 27.

Two "new" guitars provided firm evidence of CBS wringing every last drop of potential income from unused factory stock that would otherwise have been written off. The shortlived Custom (also known as Maverick) and Swinger (or Musiclander) were assembled from modified leftovers.

The Custom used discontinued Electric XII necks and bodies, converted to six-string use and with slightly reshaped body and headstock. The Swinger was made from unused Musicmaster or Bass V bodies that were mated with unpopular short-scale Mustang necks, again with the body reworked, and with the headstock turned into a spear-like point.

Both were made in necessarily limited numbers. The Swinger never featured in Fender's sales material, but was a low-end model at any price. The Custom was a little more evident, listing at $299.50 – a few dollars more than a regular Telecaster of the period.

Leo Fender's services had been retained by CBS as "special consultant in research and development." CBS didn't want Leo taking his ideas elsewhere, but equally didn't want him getting in the way of the newly efficient Fender business machine. So he was set up away from the main operation and allowed to tinker as much as he liked – with very little effect on the Fender product lines.

A couple of years after the sale to CBS, Leo recovered from his illness that had provoked the sale of Fender in the first place. He completed a few projects for CBS, but would leave when his five-year contract expired in 1970. He went on to make instruments for the Music Man company (originally set up in 1972, though not named Music Man until 1974) and his G&L operation (founded in 1979). Leo Fender died in 1991. But Leo had not been the first of the old guard to leave CBS. As we've seen, Forrest White departed in 1967 in the midst of arguments over the solid state amps. White died in 1994. Don Randall resigned from CBS in 1969, disenchanted with corporate life, and formed Randall Electric Instruments, which he sold in 1987. He died in 2008. George Fullerton left CBS in 1970, worked at Ernie Ball for a while, and with Leo formed the G&L company in 1979, although Fullerton sold his interest in 1986. (G&L at first stood for "George & Leo.") Fullerton died in 2009.

As the close of the 1960s loomed, Stratocasters took a boost when an inspired guitarist by the name of Jimi Hendrix applied the guitar's sensuous curves and glorious tone to his live cavorting and studio experiments. Fender salesman Dale Hyatt: "When guys like that came along, we couldn't build enough guitars. As a matter of fact, I think Jimi Hendrix caused more Stratocasters to be sold than all the Fender salesmen put together."

● *Main guitar: This Custom
was made in 1970.*

*Fender's 1969 ad (right) shows the
Custom alongside some striped
Competition Mustangs and a Tele
with an f-hole, the new Thinline. The
Swinger (red 1969 example, below)
was another CBS "bitser" made from
leftover parts. The headstock shape
would turn up 16 years later on
Fender's Performer. Fender's 1969
catalog (right) had it covered: from
banjos to solid-state amplifiers, from
flat-tops to f-holes.*

"Fender survived the 1970s by shunning innovation, concentrating instead on the production of its core models in vast quantities."

70s

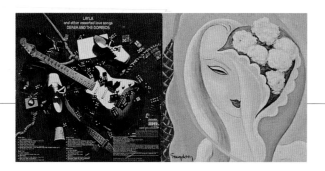

As Fender entered the 1970s there was little sign of successful innovation. Instead, management seemed increasingly content to settle on old designs and allow those to provide the major income. It was a time of musical change, too, as the heady experimentation of the 1960s subsided and pop music itself divided into yet more factions. Many would later look back on the 1970s as the least satisfying decade in Fender's history, yet as we shall see there was still much to intrigue and fascinate.

In 1966, the New York-based Ampeg company had launched the first fretless bass guitar. The instrument's smooth, unfretted fingerboard enabled bassists to achieve a sound completely different to that of the fretted instrument. Notes "swell" with a beautifully warm tone, and the fretless player can more easily execute slides. Among the earliest well-known players of fretless bass guitar was Rick Danko of American folk-rock pioneers The Band. Danko primarily played fretted Fenders, but was given some instruments by Ampeg around 1970, including a fretless bass which he quickly modified with Fender pickups. Perhaps it was this that finally spurred Fender to offer a fretless version of the Precision Bass from 1970, at the same price ($293.50) as the regular fretted model. The company also added a new bass to the bottom of its pricelist in 1970, the Musicmaster Bass, another short-scale instrument, pitched at $139.50.

The Beatles' last ever "concert" was played on the rooftop of the band's Apple HQ in London, and featured in the 1970 movie *Let It Be* that effectively charted their break-up. George Harrison played a Rosewood Telecaster, an unusual and shortlived all-rosewood model that had been launched by Fender the previous year. The exotic Rosewood Tele was made from a timber more usually regarded as suitable only for guitar fingerboards. It makes for a striking yet heavy instrument – and Fender attempted to lighten the load of later versions by moving to a two-piece construction

with hollowed chambers inside. It is said that two special Rosewood Stratocasters were also made at this time: one was a prototype; the other was apparently intended for Jimi Hendrix, but the presentation was never made.

Fender's Don Randall had been successful in securing a meeting with The Beatles at Apple some time before the famed rooftop concert. This resulted in the band receiving various Fender products: some Fender-Rhodes pianos, a Jazz Bass, and a VI six-string bass, as well as the Rosewood Tele – all of which are visible at various times during the *Let It Be* movie.

While Eric Clapton had started out with Fenders in The Yardbirds, he soon changed allegiance to Gibsons, which he used to great effect through the 1960s with John Mayall and with Cream. But when in 1970 Clapton recorded the impressive *Layla* album, the change of pace was reflected in a new choice of guitar: a Fender Stratocaster, as pictured on the back of the record's jacket (see top of page). This began a lengthy and productive relationship between Clapton and Strat, leading to a popular Fender signature model in the 1980s.

● *Main guitar: This Fretless
Precision Bass was made
about 1973.*

*George Harrison (right)
played a Rosewood
Telecaster (1969 example,
below) in The Beatles' famous
rooftop appearance in the
1970 movie Let It Be.*

*The Musicmaster Bass was also
sold as a set with a matching amp,
as in the 1970 catalog pictured
(right). Another catalog and a
pricelist from this year (opposite
and far right) show that Fender's
relatively stylish approach to
promo material was still in place at
the start of the 1970s.*

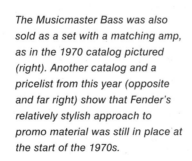

Thinlines and neck-tilts

Fender was not yet finished with the idea of a guitar that strayed into Gibson territory. However, the Thinline Telecaster ended up pleasing neither Fender nor Gibson aficionados, and did not survive the 1970s. Alterations were aimed at the Strat, which gained a three-bolt neck fixing and "bullet" truss-rod adjuster, while the number of players attracted to this and Fender's other classics was increasing all the time.

It had become obvious to the management at CBS/Fender that the experiments with hollowbody guitars – the flat-tops, electric thinline Coronados, and full-body Montego and LTD – had not been successful. Most had by now been quietly dropped from the line.

However, the company had pressed forward with another plan to gain some of the market from rivals such as Gibson who were dominating hollowbody electrics. This time, Fender took one of its finest existing models, the Telecaster, and produced a Thinline version, beginning in 1968. Roger Rossmeisl's Thinline Telecaster design had three hollowed-out cavities inside the body and a modified pickguard shaped to accommodate the single, token f-hole. At first the instrument retained the regular Telecaster pickup layout – one single-coil at the neck, plus another in the distinctive slanted position on the bridge plate.

In 1971, the Thinline Telecaster was given a new pickup layout, with two new Fender humbuckers. Humbucking pickups had two coils wired in such a way that the noise often associated with single-coil pickups was cancelled. At this time most players would have thought that Fender meant single-coil pickups while Gibson meant humbucking pickups. The new humbucker-equipped f-hole Thinline Telecaster was designed to send a signal that Fender was invading Gibson territory. But it only underlined that players still wanted identifiably Fender guitars from Fender.

It was also around this time – and quite apart from Fender – that Byrds guitarist Clarence White and drummer Gene Parsons had come up with their "shoulder strap control" B-string-pull device that fitted into a Telecaster, designed to give string-bends within chords to emulate pedal-steel type sounds. Elsewhere, Fender's musical stock was high: from Eddie Hazel's slicing Strat in Funkadelic (jacket, above) to Jimmy Page's anthemic Telecaster break on Led Zeppelin's 'Stairway To Heaven' and the low-key but refined Strat work of Steve Winwood (Traffic jacket, top left).

Starting in 1971, two primary changes were made to the Stratocaster. The adjustment point for the truss-rod was moved from the body-end of the neck to the headstock, with a new "bullet"-shaped adjuster. A neck-tilt mechanism was also added to the instrument, adjustable at the neck-plate, and the neck/body joining screws – which are nearly always called bolts – were reduced in number from four to three. These were reasonable changes in themselves, but other problems due to increased production and sloppy quality control has colored the reputation of some of these 1970s Strats.

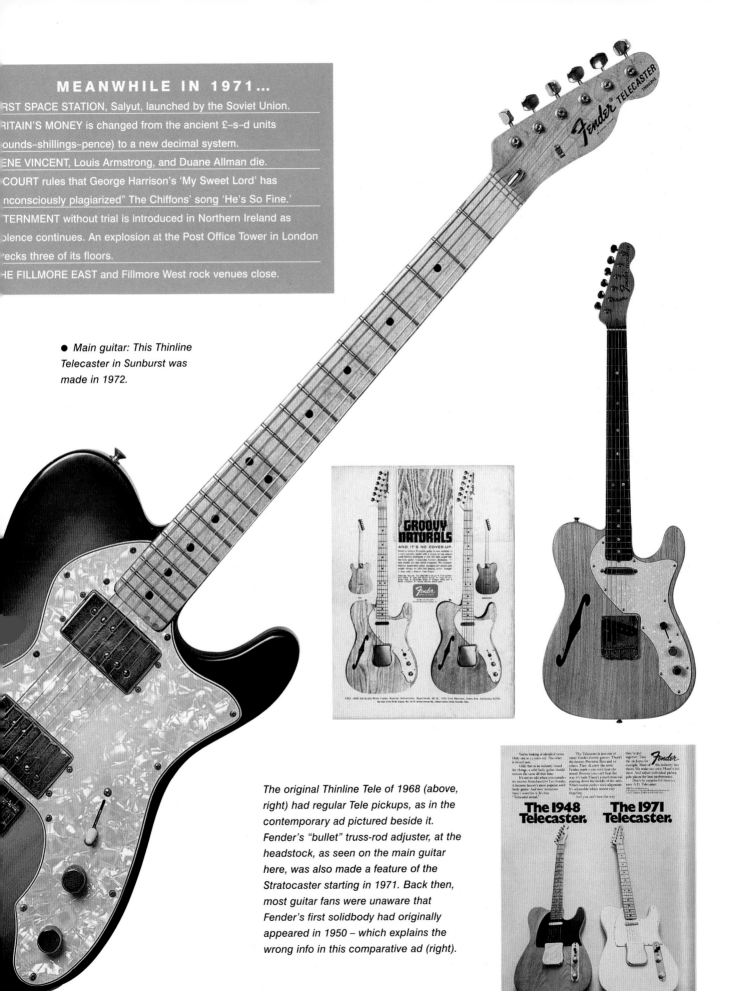

● *Main guitar: This Thinline
Telecaster in Sunburst was
made in 1972.*

*The original Thinline Tele of 1968 (above,
right) had regular Tele pickups, as in the
contemporary ad pictured beside it.
Fender's "bullet" truss-rod adjuster, at the
headstock, as seen on the main guitar
here, was also made a feature of the
Stratocaster starting in 1971. Back then,
most guitar fans were unaware that
Fender's first solidbody had originally
appeared in 1950 – which explains the
wrong info in this comparative ad (right).*

Return to bass

Humbuckers were dished out to some models, including the existing Telecaster Bass. This bass had been Fender's first reissue, designed to recreate the look of the original Precision. Now, however, the Tele Bass was saddled with one of the new humbuckers. A new Martin-like look was adopted for the Japanese-made F series flat-tops (catalog cover, right) that had debuted at the end of the 1960s, and Strat-lover Richard Thompson's first solo LP appeared (above).

Taking a look back to the original styling of the Precision Bass, Fender had come up with the Telecaster Bass in 1968. This was a significant occurrence, not so much for the instrument itself, but because it was the first time that Fender had effectively "reissued" an earlier design. Many more would follow.

The Telecaster Bass aped the maple neck, slim headstock, pickguard shape (if not color), control panel, and indeed virtually the entire general visual style of the original pre-1957 Precision Bass.

Quite why Fender came up with this reissue, however, remains something of a mystery. The Precision Bass was continuing to sell in very healthy numbers, and the new Telecaster Bass was actually pitched a few dollars higher. Standard-finish basses at the time listed for $356.50 (Jazz Bass), $302.50 (Telecaster), $293.50 (Precision), $239.50 (Mustang), and $139.50 (Musicmaster). To clutter a price-point with two models in this way was unlike Fender. Perhaps it was simply an example of an instrument that seemed like a good idea at the time?

Whatever the motivation, Fender changed the look of the Telecaster Bass in 1972 by adding one of the new humbucking pickups, a pair of which had been added to the Thinline Tele last year. The new-look Tele Bass now had little in common with the original-look Precision, and the idea of reissuing classic Fender designs went back on the shelf for some time. Fender reconsidered the effect of its wholesale replacement of single-coil pickups with humbuckers on the Thinline Tele, and came up with a different arrangement for the Telecaster Custom in 1972. This time the classic Tele lead pickup, mounted in the bridge-plate, stayed put, and just the neck pickup was changed to a humbucker – which was a relatively common modification at the time for some players who wanted a wider range of sounds from their Telecasters.

Like many Fenders of the period, the Telecaster Custom was fitted with a bullet truss-rod adjuster and the neck-tilt system. It also came with the company's new high-gloss "thick skin" finish, achieved by spraying more than a dozen coats of polyester on to the unfortunate instrument, and today much despised by some for its plastic appearance and giveaway 1970s vibe. Some models in the line were also offered in Natural ash as a Custom Color from 1972.

Blues-rock was still alive and well, and one of its finest exponents and an international blues hero was Ireland's Rory Gallagher. His battered 1961 Strat (pictured opposite) was his trademark guitar, the original sunburst body down to bare wood almost everywhere, with a much-refretted fingerboard that responded perfectly to Gallagher's nimble fingers. The guitarist continued to promote the blues with an intense passion until his untimely death in 1995.

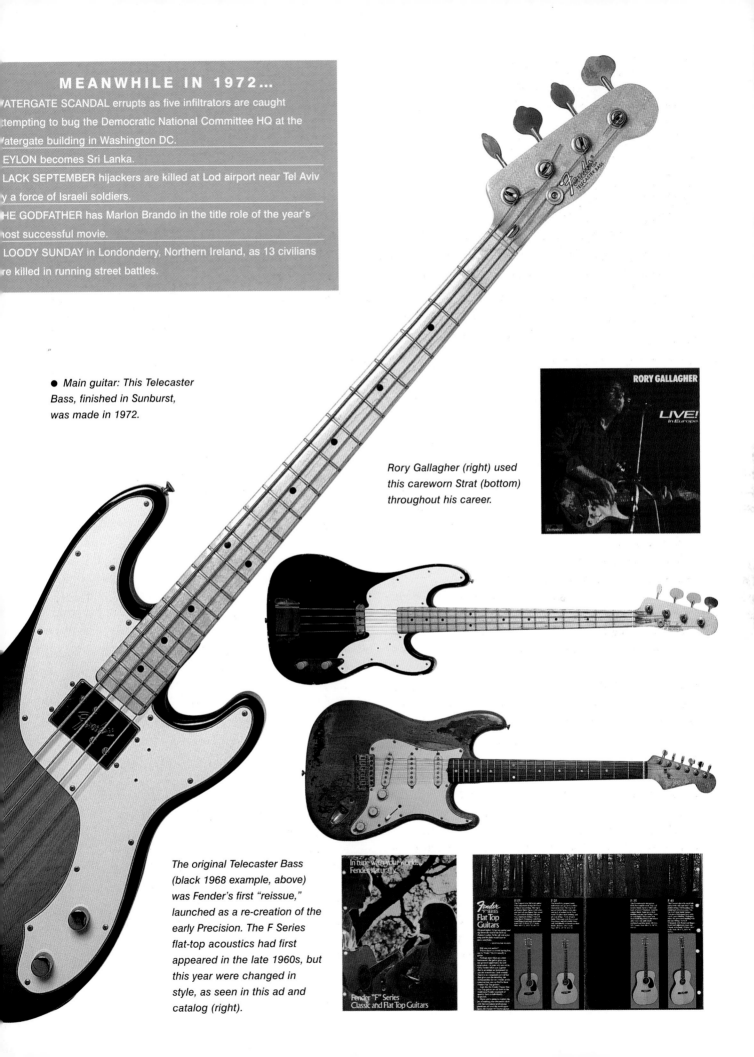

● *Main guitar: This Telecaster Bass, finished in Sunburst, was made in 1972.*

Rory Gallagher (right) used this careworn Strat (bottom) throughout his career.

The original Telecaster Bass (black 1968 example, above) was Fender's first "reissue," launched as a re-creation of the early Precision. The F Series flat-top acoustics had first appeared in the late 1960s, but this year were changed in style, as seen in this ad and catalog (right).

Numbers or quality?

As guitars poured out of Fullerton, great music continued to be fueled by Fenders. Spoilt for choice, we'll pluck just two of the great albums from this year. The Isley Brothers made *3+3* (right), featuring Ernie Isley's flowing, Hendrix-flavored Strat weaving its way among the songs, while *Countdown To Ecstasy* by Steely Dan (opposite) had guitarists Denny Dias and Jeff Baxter dueling brilliantly on Strats and Teles and more.

Part of Fender's distinction had come from using bright-sounding single-coil pickups. The warmer, fatter-sounding humbucking types were always seen then as a mainstay of Fender's principal rival, Gibson. Nonetheless, as we've seen over the last few years, Fender tried to keep abreast of changing market trends, and various models had been fitted with humbuckers. Fender had in fact hired a key Gibson engineer to devise its new humbucking pickups. Seth Lover had been enticed to California in 1967, away from the Gibson company in Michigan where Lover had famously invented Gibson's humbucking pickup in the 1950s. Warm, powerful humbuckers had given a distinctive edge to dozens of Gibson models, not least the Les Paul electrics which had come back into fashion during the late 1960s. Seth Lover found that his new employers effectively wanted an exact soundalike copy of a Gibson humbucking pickup. No surprise there.

The patent had not quite run out, so Lover designed for Fender a pickup that looked slightly different – it had staggered sets of three poles visible on the cover, as opposed to the straight line of six poles seen on a Gibson cover. Lover also took into account Fender's inclination to a brighter sound by keeping a little more brilliance in the Fender pickup's tone than there was in the Gibson.

Another new recipient of the Fender humbucker was the Telecaster Deluxe of 1973. This seemed like a cross between the big-headstocked neck and the vibrato of a

Strat, the body of a Tele, and the pickups and controls of a Gibson. Potential customers were generally confused, and at the time stayed away from the Deluxe. But they certainly did not stay away from many of Fender's other models. Marketing director David Gupton announced that 1972 had been a record year for Fender, with unit production and dollar sales figures both higher than ever before. He was in little doubt that 1973 would be higher still, and that the trend would continue upward. A major expansion program was on at the Fullerton plant to boost output still further.

This is precisely why CBS had purchased Fender back in 1965. But the increase in instruments leaving the factory inevitably affected quality. A feeling was beginning to set in that Fenders were not made like they used to be. This, coupled with a number of leading musicians regularly seen playing old guitars – now described as "vintage" instruments – added to the growing impression that numbers might be more important to Fender than quality.

STEELY DAN
countdown to ecstasy

● *Main guitar: This Telecaster Deluxe, in Sunburst finish, was made about 1976.*

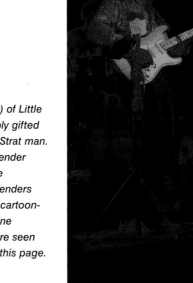

Lowell George (right) of Little Feat was a remarkably gifted guitarist and a keen Strat man. The promo men at Fender decided to stress the favoritism afforded Fenders with a new series of cartoon-inspired ads, three fine examples of which are seen along the bottom of this page.

Slap that bass

Production lines were still jammed on full throttle, churning out hundreds of instruments a day. They fell into some talented funky hands, few more exciting than those of Larry Graham (left). The ex-Sly & The Family Stone bassman defined slap funk on his Jazz Bass, and formed Graham Central Station, whose startling first album (right) was out this year.

The catalog of guitars and basses was by 1974 beginning to settle down to a revised pattern. After the cold reception for the recent spate of "new" humbucker-equipped models, Fender's taste for fresh designs slackened off considerably.

A glance at the chronology assembled at the rear of this book tells its own story about the singular lack of new models in the 1970s. It's clear that Fender was quite sensibly concentrating in general on its strengths – and as a result was enjoying its most successful period, producing a greater quantity of instruments than it had ever done in its entire history.

Remaining at the top of the line for solidbody electrics was the Jaguar, at $460 in sunburst, closely followed by the Jazzmaster at $430. Strats came with various specs including maple neck, "hardtail" (no vibrato), and left-handed choices, with the regular rosewood-fingerboard sunburst model priced at $380. A further $18 would secure you a Custom Color Strat, now down to a sorry list of blond, white, black, natural, or walnut. Custom Colors were discontinued altogether this year for Jag and Jazzmaster. You could have sunburst or sunburst, to misquote Henry Ford. No doubt Henry would have been impressed by the mass-production on display at Fullerton.

As you continued to glance at the pricelist so thoughtfully tucked into your 1970s catalog, you'd notice that Telecasters came in a similar array of specs such as maple neck and left-handers, and also with a Bigsby vibrato option. However, a regular rosewood-'board blond Tele was pitched at $295, plus $15 if you could find a Custom Color that took your fancy. The basic Tele Deluxe in Walnut was $410; the Tele Custom $325; and Tele Thinline $385. Three budget guitars completed the line: the $229 Mustang, $189 Bronco, and $172 Musicmaster. The bass list was headed by the Jazz, with maple neck or left-hand options, retailing at $366 for the standard rosewood-fingerboard model (plus $18 for Custom Color: blond, white, black, natural, or walnut). The Telecaster Bass was still there, at $312 for a blond, followed by the Precision in quite a number of options including maple neck, narrow neck, fretless and left-hand. The regular rosewood-board sunburst Precision Bass sold for $305, plus $14 for the same limited set of Custom Colors as the Jazz. Rounding off the bass catalog was the Bass VI at $387, Mustang for $249, and Musicmaster at $149.

One more sign of the vastly increased production at Fender was the cessation of neck dates. Since the earliest days of Esquires and Broadcasters, workers had almost always pencilled and later rubber-stamped dates on the body-end of necks. It's about the most reliable way to date a Fender – leaving aside the question of fakes. But from 1973 to the early 1980s Fender stopped doing it. Too busy, presumably.

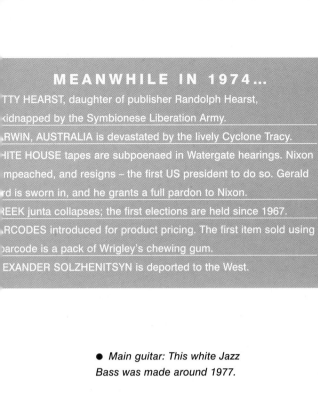

● *Main guitar: This white Jazz Bass was made around 1977.*

Proto-funk band The Meters relied on the solid groove of Fender-fancier Leo Nocentelli on albums such as Rejuvenation (above).

Speed, decided Fender's ever-busy promo people, was of the essence in a new series of ads.

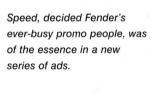

1975
Bronze metal

Fender's instruments were being sold in over 3,000 music stores throughout the world, and in the US alone there were 19 salesmen dedicated to Fender promotion. Leo Fender was long gone from the company, but his name was being used on a vast number of products ranging from Leo's original lines – steel guitars and amplifiers – to PA equipment, electric pianos and, of course, electric guitars.

The UK distributor of Fender was CBS/Arbiter, a joint venture formed with Ivor Arbiter who had been the company's British agent since the mid 1960s when he'd taken over from Jennings and Selmer. Arbiter had opened the Fender Soundhouse, a new instrument superstore in London's Tottenham Court Road, toward the end of 1973.

Sculptor Jon Douglas had been working at Arbiter's house, and was invited to visit the store. When he noted that most of the guitars looked "boring," Arbiter invited him to do better. Douglas came up with a replacement Stratocaster body made from cold-cast bronze, employing a metallic layer over a fiberglass shell. A prototype (pictured opposite) was made, followed by six more models. Each had the sculpted body, in a variety of shades, and after a suggestion from Arbiter rhinestones were set into the body's surface, providing the instrument's name. This small batch of Rhinestone Stratocasters was put on sale at the Soundhouse in 1975, but unfortunately a fire destroyed the premises soon afterward. It would seem that two of the "production" models had already been sold, but the other four are likely to have perished in the flames. Douglas made fresh molds for a further run of around 25 examples in the early 1990s, some adapting old 1970s parts, others with modern components, and all identified by a numbered plaque set into the molding on the rear of the body.

As 1970s Stratocasters with replacement bodies,

original Rhinestone Strats might fail to excite collectors of vintage axes. But the connection with Jon Douglas, who continued to work as a sculptor before his death in the 1990s, certainly make them significant as the first Fender "art" guitars.

Over in California, not much was changing in the Fender lines. A little fiddling was done to the budget-price Musicmaster guitar, and the Jazz Bass was brought into line with the other models that had adopted the tilt-neck system, "bullet" truss-rod adjuster at the headstock, and three-bolt neck fixing.

Musical highlights from Fender players included the great Bruce Springsteen album *Born To Run*, with Bruce memorably pictured clutching his trusty Esquire on the jacket (top) alongside saxman Clarence Clemons. Springsteen's lead guitarist, Miami Steve Van Zandt, was often seen with a Strat, as was Nils Lofgren, who would join Springsteen's band in later years. Lofgren's first solo album (opposite) was out this year, and it showcased the talents of the ex-Neil Young musician, not only as a gifted composer but also as an inventive and inspired guitarist.

● *Main guitar: This Rhinestone
Stratocaster prototype was
made in 1975.*

*Fairy tales were the next
source of inspiration for
Fender's developing ad series.
This wild jam (above left)
seems to feature Alice and
The Three Bears. Aston
Barrett (right) was the brilliant
Jazz-toting reggae bassman in
Bob Marley's Wailers. The
band's fine Live! and Natty
Dread LPs were out this year.*

Casting the star

The guitar R&D department broke a three-year silence to introduce a new model, the hollowbody Starcaster, but it still failed to improve the company's performance alongside Gibson's hollowbody electrics, and the model was gone from the catalog in less than four years. New pedal-steels (right) included Artist and Student models. The most notable players who were forging ahead with Fender instruments this year were Jeff Beck (above) and Jaco Pastorius (opposite page).

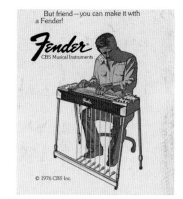

The Starcaster was another attempt to lure guitarists away from their Gibson thinline hollowbody electrics. Launched in 1976, it was a much better instrument than some of the previous hollowbody models, but still failed to excite players. The project started life as another of CBS's attempts to use old stock, as they had done with the previous Custom and Swinger. But early prototypes were too obviously outings for scrap components from Coronados, so management gave designer Gene Fields the go-ahead to come up with a completely new guitar. The result was a hollowbody electric more in keeping with Fender's overall style, bearing an offset-waist body and a Fender-like headstock.

Despite the inherent quality of the $850 Starcaster, its timing was wrong, and most potential customers still opted for Gibson hollowbody models. Later on, Fender decided not to waste valuable Strat and Tele production time on the Starcaster, and the guitar had left the list by 1980.

The new Super Twin amp marked the high point of a trend towards power: it produced no less than 180 watts from within a regular-size 2x12 combo cabinet. Visually the model was in contrast to the "silverface" look prevalent at Fender at the time, and adopted a black control panel that hinted at the old (and today revered) "blackface" style. The new amp had done well in the laboratory but never managed to attract many real-world players to its fulsome charms.

Jeff Beck had gone back to using a Gibson Les Paul for his acclaimed 1975 jazz-rock album *Blow By Blow*, but for the fine follow-up *Wired* (top of page) the guitarist took up Strats once more – and has stayed faithful on almost every recording since.

Another influential Fender player was Jaco Pastorius, whose astonishing solo album (opposite) came out this year. Pastorius popularized the sound of fretless bass, playing his de-fretted Jazz Bass (as well as a regular fretted Jazz) in a virtuosic manner as a featured instrument. The album included the impressively double-tracked 'Continuum' that defined the Jaco fretless sound. A year later, Pastorius would join jazz-rock group Weather Report, staying on for six eventful years and still further enhancing the appeal of the fretless.

Fender's serial-numbering system changed this year to the style still used today. From 1976, the first few characters of most US serials show the approximate year of manufacture. An initial letter is for a decade – S for 1970s, E for 1980s, N for 1990s, Z for 2000s, and T for 2010 and later. The following digit fixes the year; but from 2010 this is a separate two-digit prefix. There are some anomalies, but these systems do offer a fair guide to production period.

● *Main guitar: This natural-
finish Starcaster was made
around 1978.*

Fender stayed with the earlier fairy-tale theme for its
ads, and now had Snow White and the Witch (above)
getting down to a Starcaster-led groove. The company
had used the Tarrega brandname for some classical
guitars in the 1960s, but by now (below, left) they used
it for a line of strings. A further series of inventive ads
this year (two are pictured below) had guitars and
amps frightening the wildlife.

Inbetweenies

The production onslaught that continued into this year at Fender's busy Fullerton factories was designed to supply a demand for the company's gear across a wide range of musical tastes – and the revived Antigua shaded finish did at least bring some brightness to a depleted list of Custom Colors. Meanwhile, Televison's debut album *Marquee Moon* (above) was released this year, with Tom Verlaine's brilliant Jazzmaster work right up front and unmissable.

A shortlived revival began this year of the Antigua finish, the light-to-dark shaded color that had first been offered as an option during the late 1960s on some of the Coronado models. Back then, the finish had been adopted as an emergency measure to disguise manufacturing flaws. But this time around it was deployed purely for its aesthetic appeal.

Fender's list of Custom Colors had been pared right back, and the new-style Antigua at least offered some brightness among a somewhat dowdy list of around half a dozen options. Models available in Antigua were the standard Strat and Tele, plus the Telecaster Deluxe and Custom, the Mustang and Mustang Bass, and the Jazz and Precision Bass. This new Antigua style, now with more of a graduated tone, was matched to similarly finished pickguards.

Also featured on the new Antigua guitars was the new black hardware that Fender had started to use from 1975. All the plasticware – knobs, pickup covers, switch caps and all – was now black, and this certainly enhanced the overall look of the Antigua-finish instruments. It was also around this time that Fender's tuners were generally replaced by closed-cover units bought in from the German Schaller company, a supplier used until 1983.

Cut-backs in the electric guitar line had been continuing: the Duo-Sonic had been dropped in 1969; the last Esquire of the period was made in 1970; and the Jaguar had disappeared around 1975. On the Stratocaster, Fender began to fit a five-way selector switch from 1977, replacing the old three-way unit.

From its launch in 1954 the Strat bore a selector pickup switch that offered three firm settings: neck pickup, or middle pickup, or bridge pickup. Later, some players began to discover that if the switch was lodged precariously between the "official" settings, combinations of pickups became available.

Lodging the three-way switch between neck and middle settings gave those two pickups combined, and similarly for middle and bridge. There was also a change to the quality of the sound in these in-between positions, caused by phase cancellation and producing "hollow" or "honky" sounds – as well as a volume decrease – that could be quite useful musically.

Players would sometimes loosen the spring inside the switch to make it easier to lodge the switch at in-between settings. Some accessory manufacturers spotted the trend and began to offer replacement five-way switches that gave the standard three positions plus two firm, "clickable" settings for the new sounds. It took Fender until 1977 to change the standard switch on the Stratocaster to a five-way unit. The guitarist probably most identified with the "hollowed-out" sounds of the inbetweenies was Mark Knopfler of Dire Straits, whose debut album of 1978 would be awash with the sounds of phase-cancelled Strat pickups.

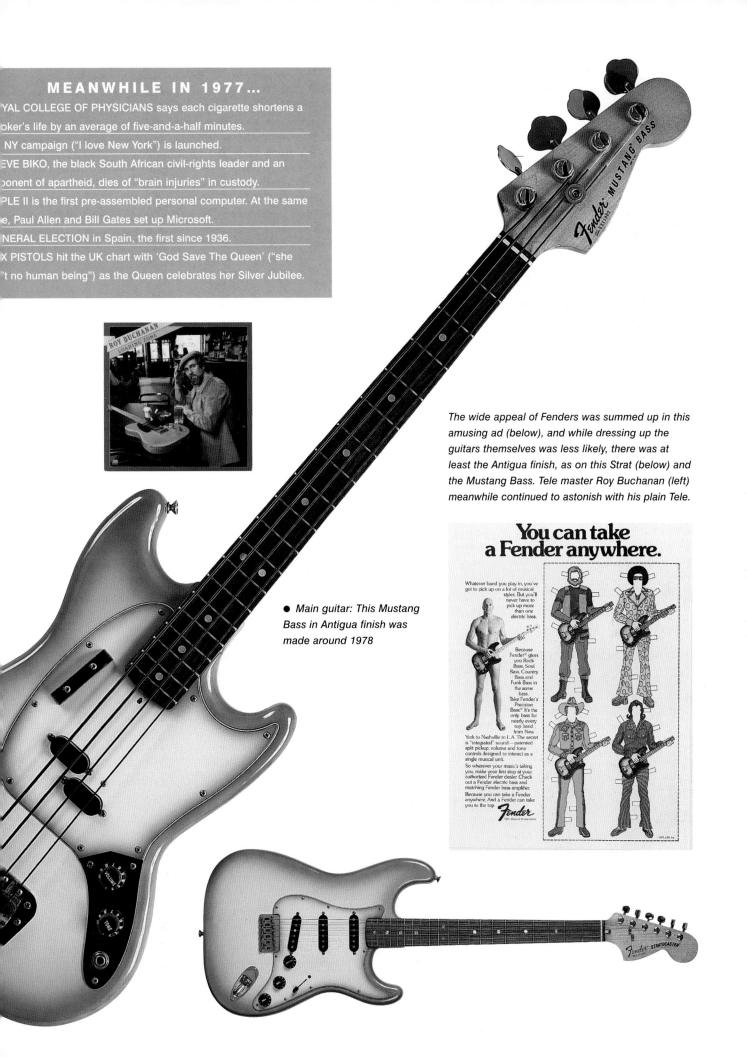

The wide appeal of Fenders was summed up in this amusing ad (below), and while dressing up the guitars themselves was less likely, there was at least the Antigua finish, as on this Strat (below) and the Mustang Bass. Tele master Roy Buchanan (left) meanwhile continued to astonish with his plain Tele.

● *Main guitar: This Mustang Bass in Antigua finish was made around 1978*

1978
Lost in music

At the Fender factories, hundreds of new guitars were being packed for  **shipping every day. They became the raw material for musicians intent on discovering yet more ways of broadening the scope of pop music. Punk was becoming new wave. Dance music had fractured into disco, funk and soul. And rock was facing an identity crisis, forced to adopt parallel roles as jazz-rock, country-rock, heavy-rock, and more.**

To survey key Fender players during the late 1970s is to underline the sheer diversity of popular music at the time. Some of it was startlingly good, some embarrassingly bad, some simply pathetic. But the fan of the time could hardly complain about lack of choice. Guitarists were worried that the newly popular keyboard synthesizer might devalue and even eclipse the electric guitar in pop, but eventually it settled alongside the other instruments. Although the sonic possibilities for the guitar were now virtually limitless with modern amps and effects, Fender's traditionally bright sound was well positioned to cut through a band that might now include synths and drum machines as much as the more usual components.

Some great debut albums appeared this year: The Police (right) had Andy Summers on a Tele, Sting on Precision; Dire Straits meant Mark Knopfler (opposite, top left) and a cleanly flowing Strat; and Chic's Nile Rodgers (left) often used a Strat for his insistent and irresistible grooves.

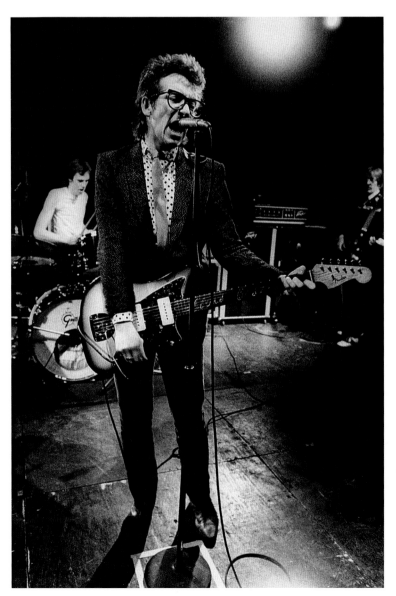

Elvis Costello with Jazzmaster (left); Frank Zappa (below) and flambéed ex-Hendrix Strat; and an all-Fender song for Talking Heads (opposite).

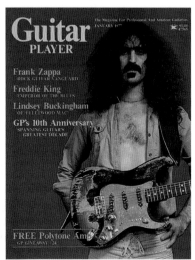

1979
Anniversary schmaltz

As the 1970s closed, Fender made its first anniversary model, to mark 25 years of the Strat, but little beyond the dated neckplate on the back of the body connected the instrument with the mid 1950s. It was almost as if CBS was underlining the fact that Fender back then was a whole world away from the modern firm. Down at the bottom of the pricelist, two new budget Lead models made a brief appearance, with the Lead III (above) making it a trio a few years later.

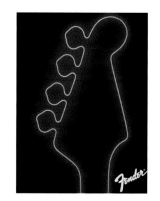

This year marked the 25th anniversary of the introduction of the Stratocaster, and Fender decided to celebrate the occasion with its first-ever anniversary model. Today, we might expect a nit-picking replica accurate enough to satisfy the most anal of collectors. Not so in 1979.

About the only concessions to the design specifics of a 1954 Strat were the fretted maple neck and body-end truss-rod adjustment. Otherwise what you got was a 1979 Stratocaster with a unique paint job, a cheesy Anniversary logo on the upper horn, a celebratory neck-plate with special serial number, and locking Sperzel tuners.

Fender shifted during 1979 from its multi-coat "thick skin" polyester finish to a water-based paint. The earliest examples of the 25th Anniversary Strat used the new finish, in Pearl White. Unfortunately this cracked spectacularly. Most were sent back to the factory from irate stores or owners, and Fender reverted to polyester paints. The main production of the 25th Anniversary was changed to a more appropriate silver finish.

"The quantity, naturally, is limited," announced Fender... who during 1979 and 1980 proceeded to make thousands of 25th Anniversary Stratocasters ($800 including case, virtually the same price as a standard model). "They went fast in '54. They'll go fast now," ran the insistent ad. An official estimate of production mentioned some 10,000 units.

The model 75 amp came out this year, incorporating some influences from the MESA Boogie amps that caused a stir at the time. Boogies had popularized the master volume control, which provided more precise overdrive/distortion control, and channel switching, for selecting between clean and overdrive channels by using a footswitch. Fender's 75 adopted these features, as well as some technical trickery to provide overdrive at a switchable lower power.

Gregg Wilson in R&D landed the job of designing a new pair of "student" models, intended eventually to replace the Musicmaster, Bronco, and Mustang that sat at the bottom of the company's six-string pricelist at the time. Wilson's new guitars were the Lead I and Lead II, introduced in 1979. They were simple, double-cutaway solidbodies, but ended up not especially cheap at $399. For the time being, the original budget trio remained: the Mustang retailing for $450, the Bronco $340, and the Musicmaster $320 (all these prices including a case). John Page, whom we'll meet again later in this book, designed a variation, the Lead III of 1981 – but none of the Lead guitars lasted beyond 1982.

Apparently there was a joke often heard around Fender at the time: "We don't build them like we used to... and we never did." CBS was selling 40,000 Fender instruments a year by the end of the 1970s.

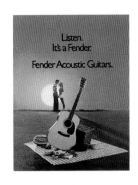

● *Main guitar: This 25th Anniversary
Stratocaster, finished in 25th
Anniversary Silver, was made in 1979.*

*The new budget Lead I and Lead II
models were featured in the new
catalog (bottom). Robert Smith of The
Cure (below) is a long-time Jazzmaster
fan, and his spikey guitar work was
strongly featured on the band's debut
LP this year.*

the eighties

"Diversification was the key to this Fender decade, with fresh models, Japanese production, signature guitars, and a new Custom Shop."

80s

Omit ocaster

Signs appeared of a realization that some Fenders might be out of touch with current trends. The Stratocaster and the Precision Bass were given a makeover, creating alongside the regular models the new Precision Special Bass (right) and Strat. Quite happy with the existing fare were the architects of heavy rock, Iron Maiden (Dave Murray, Stratocaster, and Steve Harris, P-bass, pictured opposite), who impressed with their debut LP, out this year.

Most people tend to refer to a Stratocaster as a "Strat," and in 1980 Fender finally used the abbreviation officially on a new model designed by Gregg Wilson. It was Wilson who had come up with the budget Lead models, introduced the previous year.

Fender's new Strat combined standard Stratocaster looks with updated circuitry, a "hot" bridge pickup, and fashionable, heavy-duty brass hardware. The latter was also offered by Fender as Original Brass Works after-market accessories, following the lead of various companies who had popularized a craze for retrofit replacement parts. Larry DiMarzio had been in the forefront of this new business, introducing his Super Distortion replacement pickup in 1975, with Mighty Mite, Seymour Duncan and others following soon.

Fender also intended with the Strat to re-introduce the old-style narrow headstock of the original Stratocasters – the larger type of the time had been in use since around 1965 – but as old worn-out tooling was used the result was not an entirely accurate re-creation. Smaller, certainly; accurate, no. A reversion to the four-bolt neck fixing, body-end truss-rod adjustment, and removal of the neck-tilt for the new Strat also implied that CBS were already aware of criticisms of 1970s Stratocasters.

A few brighter colors were offered for the Strat, too, reviving Lake Placid Blue, Candy Apple Red, and Olympic White. The Strat retailed at $995, compared to $745 for a regular Stratocaster of the time. A similar makeover provided a new option to the regular Precision, the Precision Special Bass. Brass hardware, body-end truss-rod adjuster, brighter colors and the rest were there, plus a switchable active circuit. Again, this indicated that CBS had an eye on current trends.

Active electronics meant wider tonal potential thanks to an on-board pre-amp. The bassist was able to boost treble and bass tones on an active bass, whereas normal "passive" circuits can only cut from existing tones. California maker Alembic had done much to publicize active basses during the 1970s, but probably more galling for CBS was Leo Fender's superb active bass guitar, the StingRay, launched by his new Music Man operation in 1976. Both the Strat and Precision Special would last in the Fender line until 1983.

One further attempt this year to provide something different for Stratocaster fans was the Hendrix Stratocaster, which turned out to be a very limited run indeed. This was something like a 25th Anniversary Strat in overall spec, but with an inverted headstock and additional body contouring, and only in white. It's significant as the first Fender made to highlight an association with a musician – a sales technique that would become very important to the company from the late 1980s – but only 25 or so were actually produced.

MEANWHILE IN 1980...

IRANIAN EMBASSY seized in London; two hostages killed. SAS
storm building, release hostages, and kill all but one gunman.

WAR breaks out between Iran and Iraq.

EIGHT AMERICAN servicemen are killed in an unsuccessful
attempt to free US hostages held in Iran.

RONALD REAGAN is elected US president.

JOHN LENNON is murdered in New York City. Also dead this year:
Peter Sellers, John Bonham, Jean-Paul Sartre, Mantovani, Henry
Miller, and Professor Longhair.

CONSERVATIONISTS protest at dolphin slaughter in Japan.

● *Main guitar: This Strat,
finished in Lake Placid Blue,
was made in 1980.*

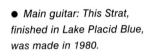

*The new Strat in two promo items:
a 1980 ad (left) and a 1981 catalog
(opposite page, top) that shows a
Stratocaster, a Strat, and a
Stratocaster, top to bottom. Dave
Murray (above) and Steve Harris of
Iron Maiden aim their Fender
weapons carefully.*

Part Tele. Part Strat. All Excitement: The Affordable Fender Bullets.

In with the new

A turning point occurred as new management was installed by CBS. The owners had clearly been rattled by Fender's recent tendency to follow rather than lead the world in instrument fashions. Several new men from Yamaha's US operation were hired, and the changes were felt relatively quickly as, for example, a new-specification Stratocaster Standard was launched on to the market.

CBS management decided that new blood was needed to help reverse the decline in Fender's image. Income had been climbing spectacularly to 1980, tripling in that year compared to 1971's $20 million revenues, but re-investment was wavering.

During 1981 key personnel were recruited from the US-based instrument arm of the giant Japanese company Yamaha. John McLaren was brought in to head up CBS Musical Instruments overall, Bill Schultz was the new Fender president, and Dan Smith was director of marketing electric guitars. Schultz was given the go-ahead by CBS to try to improve matters.

Briefly available was a new set of Custom Colors known as International Colors, illustrated in the 1981 catalog (opposite), intended to make existing stock more attractive. However, many of the hues were distinctly lurid – as indicated by the Capri Orange Stratocaster pictured (opposite) alongside a more reserved Sahara Taupe model. They were not liked at the time. (The Sahara Taupe Stratocaster shown is an oddity in itself as the neck has a four-screw fixing and no "bullet" on the large headstock, indicating it may originally have been intended for a 25th Anniversary.)

One of the first changes Dan Smith made was to revise the Strat's overall specs, introducing the Stratocaster Standard as the new regular model. It reverted to body-end truss-rod adjustment, a revamped narrow headstock shape, and what was generally felt to be the more stable four-screw

neck/body fixing. (The cover of the 1981 catalog – pictured above – was printed before the changes and shows the earlier "large" headstock.) Schultz recommended a large investment package, primarily aimed at modernizing the factory. This had the immediate effect of virtually stopping production while new machinery was brought in and staff was re-trained.

John Page in R&D provided the next generation of budget-price solidbodies with 1981's single-cutaway Bullet series. The Bronco and Musicmaster had been dropped in 1980, the Mustang in 1981. Fender decided for the first time in its history to shift manufacturing outside the United States, aiming to eliminate tooling costs. Joining a general trend in the early 1980s among many guitar companies both Western and Eastern, Fender decided to try Korean manufacturing. But early samples were poor, and Fender decided not to have the Bullets made entirely in Korea.

At first Bullets were assembled in the US with Korean parts, but even this method failed to produce guitars of a high enough standard. By late 1981 the Bullets were back to full American production, and Fender's first experience of oriental manufacturing was over. The Bullets lasted until 1983, in which year various shortlived double-cutaway versions were also produced.

● *Main guitar: This Bullet, in
Red finish, was produced
around 1982.*

*Adrian Belew, known for
deploying modified Strats
and Mustangs to devastating
effect, was in fine form on
King Crimson's densely-
textured Discipline (left).*

*The ad (above) is for the later Squier Bullets,
which began to appear in 1983. Two Stratocasters
finished in the new International Colors are
pictured (below), in Sahara Taupe (left) and Capri
Orange, alongside a catalog showing the full set.*

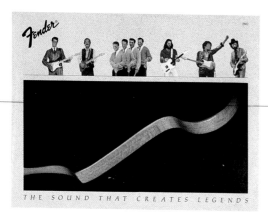

THE SOUND THAT CREATES LEGENDS

Japanese production began this year, and the first Vintage reissues were out, recreating classic models with 1950s and 1960s-period styling. The 1982 catalog (above) stressed the heritage with cover stars from Holly to Hendrix. Plenty of current stars rated Fender, too, while some aligned with other brands – such as the Rickenbacker-inclined Tom Petty (right) – often made space for a Fender.

By the dawn of the 1980s the US dollar had soared in value relative to the Japanese yen. Coupled with the high quality of many guitars being exported from dozens of increasingly skilled Japanese manufacturers, this meant that lots of players were cheerfully ignoring American-made guitars and opting for well-made, good-price instruments made in the orient.

A good deal of these instruments were copies of the Fender Stratocaster, which was enjoying renewed popularity. And the Japanese copyists were making the biggest profits in their own domestic market. So the new Fender management team looked hard at the market, and figured that the best place to hit back at them was in Japan – by making and selling guitars there. Fender would, in effect, copy itself.

So it was that negotiations began with two Japanese instrument distributors, Kanda Shokai and Yamano Music, to establish the Fender Japan company. The joint venture was officially established in March 1982. After discussions with Tokai, Kawai, and other manufacturers, the factory chosen to build guitars for Fender Japan was Fujigen. The plant was based in Matsumoto, some 130 miles north-west of Tokyo. Fujigen was best known in the West for the excellence of its Ibanez-brand instruments.

Back at Fender HQ, another part of the plan emerged. Fender would recreate the guitars that many players and collectors were spending large sums of money to acquire: the "vintage" guitars made back in

the company's glory years in the 1950s and 1960s. The Vintage reissue series began in 1982. The guitars consisted of a maple-neck '57 Stratocaster and '57 Precision Bass, a rosewood-fingerboard '62 Strat and '62 Precision, a '62 Jazz Bass, and a '52 Telecaster.

Aside from some die-hard Fender collectors, most people who saw the new guitars praised and welcomed them. Production of the Vintage models was planned to start in 1982 at Fender US (Fullerton) and Fender Japan (Fujigen), but changes being instituted at the American factory meant that some US versions did not come on-stream until early 1983.

Fender Japan's guitars at this stage were being made only for the internal Japanese market, but one of Fender's European agents was pressing for budget-price models to compete with other Japanese imports. So Fender Japan made some less costly versions of the Vintage reissues for European distribution, starting in 1982. These were distinguished at first by a small Squier Series logo on the tip of the headstock. This was soon changed, with a large Squier marque replacing the Fender logo.

Thus the Squier brand was born. The name came from a string-making company, V.C. Squier, that Fender had acquired in 1965. Victor Carroll Squier had founded his firm in 1890 in Battle Creek, Michigan. The Squier name would become increasingly valuable to Fender in the coming years.

● *Main guitar: This
Squier Series '62 Jazz
Bass, in Sunburst, was
made in 1982.*

**ROCK WITH
ESQUIER STRINGS**

The string with the snappy magnetic response. Made
of the finest alloys for prolonged playing life—precision wound for maximum resistance to stretch and
pull. Available at your nearest music dealer. For
Free String Catalog write V.C. Squire, Dept. MT-58,
427 Capitol Ave., S.W., Battle Creek, Mich. 49016

V.C. **SQUIER**
Since 1890

*An ad from the late 1960s
(left) uses Jimi Hendrix to
promote Esquier strings,
made by the Fender-owned
Squier company. The Squier
name was revived by Fender
in 1982 for a new line of
Japanese-built guitars. This
Squier Series Stratocaster
(above) was made in 1982.*

*Vintage flavors: a Squier
Series Strat (above), a '57
Precision Bass (left), and a
'52 Telecaster (top left).*

57 PRECISION BASS

ERIC CLAPTON   MONEY AND CIGARETTES

Elite complications

Change was still clearly detectable in the air this year as the Japanese-made Squier-brand guitars first went on sale in the US (ad, right) and the American-made Vintage models finally began to come off the production line ('57 Strat, opposite). A new high-end line known as the Elite Series was launched, Paul Rivera's take on solid-state amps appeared, and Eric Clapton borrowed a Strat from Salvador Dali (above).

THERE'S MAGIC IN THE BREED

The Japanese-made Squier series, introduced in 1982 and now with a large Squier logo, was put on sale this year in America. The first US Squier ad to appear (above right) majors on the Vintage Tele, Strat and P-Bass. This marked the start of the sale of Fender Japan products around the world, and the move by Fender to become an international manufacturer of guitars. It taught the new team at Fender an important lesson, and one that earlier managements would not have believed: that musicians would buy Fender guitars with "made in Japan" on them.

At one time there had certainly been a resistance by many players to the cheap image associated with Japanese-made guitars. But the rise in quality of the instruments from brands such as Ibanez, Yamaha, Fernandes, Aria, Tokai – and Fender and Squier – wiped away a good deal of this prejudice. Oriental guitars were gaining a new popularity and respectability. At the US factory this year some cost-cutting changes were made to the Standard models. The alterations were the result of the dollar's strength and the consequent difficulty in selling US-made products overseas, where they were becoming increasingly high-priced. Savings had to be made, so the Strat lost a tone control and its distinctive jack plate, while the Tele shed its tone-enhancing through-body stringing. Minor mods were also made to the Standard basses. The revisions to the six-strings were ill-conceived, and many who had applauded the

improvements made since 1981 groaned inwardly at the familiar signs of economics once again apparently taking precedence over playability and sound. Fortunately, these mutant varieties of Fender's key models lasted only until 1985.

Another shortlived series from the same period consisted of the Elite Stratocaster, Elite Telecaster, and Elite Precision Bass. These were radical new high-end versions of the old faithfuls. But the vibrato-equipped Elite Strat came saddled with a terrible bridge, which is what most players recall when the Elites are mentioned. In-fighting at Fender had led to last-minute changes and the result was an unwieldy, unworkable piece of hardware.

The Elite Strat also featured three pushbuttons for pickup selection, not to the taste of players brought up on the classic Fender switch. There were good points – the new pickups, the effective active circuitry, and the improved truss-rod design – but they tended to be overlooked. The Elites – including optional gold-hardware and walnut neck/body versions – were dropped by 1985.

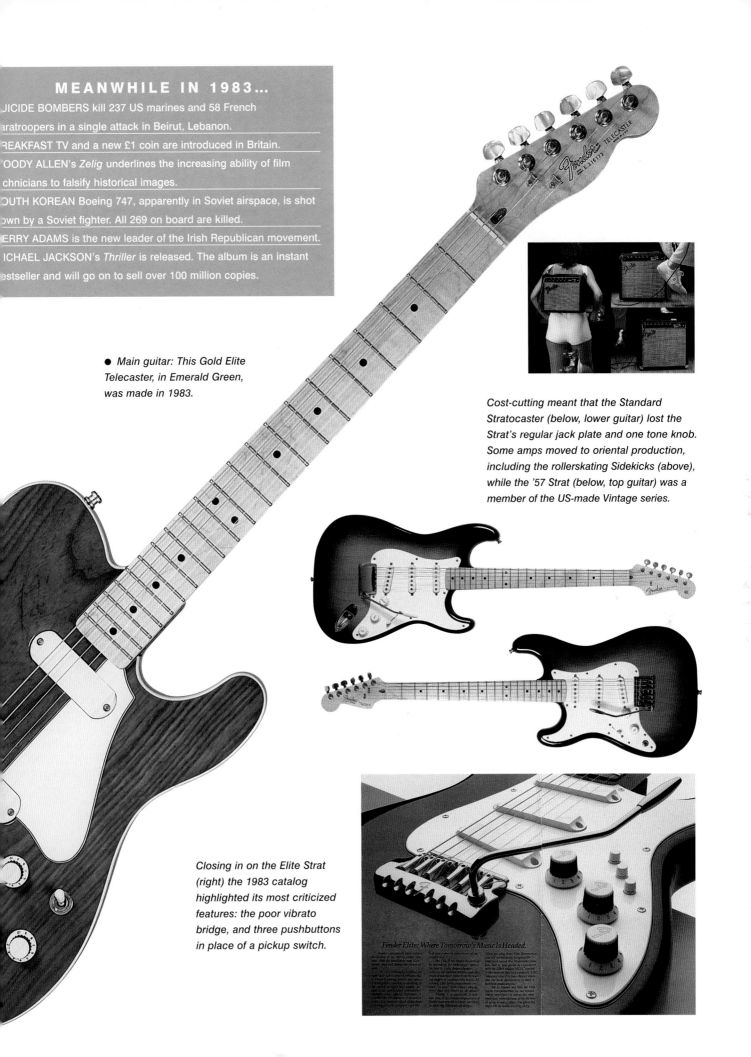

● *Main guitar: This Gold Elite Telecaster, in Emerald Green, was made in 1983.*

Cost-cutting meant that the Standard Stratocaster (below, lower guitar) lost the Strat's regular jack plate and one tone knob. Some amps moved to oriental production, including the rollerskating Sidekicks (above), while the '57 Strat (below, top guitar) was a member of the US-made Vintage series.

Closing in on the Elite Strat (right) the 1983 catalog highlighted its most criticized features: the poor vibrato bridge, and three pushbuttons in place of a pickup switch.

Fender Elite: Where Tomorrow's Music Is Headed.

1984
Turning Japanese

The new Fender Japan operation was still the main production base because the US factory's machines, systems, and staff were gradually recovering from reorganization. New models emerged from Japan – the Flame (right, top), Esprit (right, below), and D'Aquisto. Further musical diversity was evident from Fender players, as Los Lobos (above) mixed rockabilly and Tex-Mex, and Johnny Marr (opposite) underpinned the melodic pop of The Smiths.

Another colorful ploy to try to use up existing stock was the "Bowling Ball" or "Marble" finish applied to 100 or so each of the Strat and Tele Standards at the US factory. The red, yellow or blue streaked effects were striking – but not really enough to detract from the shortcomings of the guitars themselves.

On the other side of the world, the new Fender Japan operation was busy adding new models to its Vintage reissue series. This time the magnifying glass was trained on a wider portion of Fender history, and over the next few years Fender Japan would introduce remakes including 50s, 60s, and '72-style Strats, a number of the 1970s-era hubucker'd Tele models, including a '72 Custom and a '69 and '72 Thinline, and the bound-body Custom Telecaster and Esquire.

Three new-design lines were introduced in 1984, intended yet again to compete with some of Gibson's electric guitars. All were manufactured by Fender Japan, as Fender's US factory was still not back up to speed following the reorganizations that were being undertaken by the new management team brought in by CBS from Yamaha US.

The overall name for the new instruments was the Master Series, encompassing the electric hollowbody archtop D'Aquisto models – with design input from American luthier Jimmy D'Aquisto – and the semi-solid double-cutaway Esprit and Flame guitars.

The D'Aquistos were offered as the shortlived two-pickup Standard and the fancier single-pickup Elite.

The Elite lasted to the mid 1990s, when it moved to US manufacturing and changed to a floating pickup arrangement, alongside a new D'Aquisto Deluxe model with fixed single pickup.

The equal-cutaway Esprit and slightly-offset-cutaway Flame each came in three variations: Standard; Elite with fine-tuners; and Ultra with fine-tuners and gold-plated hardware.

Significantly for the continuing growth of Fender as an international manufacturer, these were the first Fender Japan products with the Fender rather than Squier headstock logo to be sold officially outside Japan. They were also the first ever Fender models to feature "set" glued-in necks rather than the company's customary bolt-on method, a further hint at competition with Gibson (who habitually employed set necks).

In fact, the overtly Gibson image of the Esprits and Flames was to be their undoing. Construction and quality were good, and sounds and playability impressive. But they weren't "Fender." Also, Fender Japan's factory, Fujigen, had problems, and stock didn't arrive for some time. And then the owners pulled the plug. After nearly 20 years, CBS finally decided they'd had enough.

● *Main guitar: This D'Aquisto
Deluxe, in Sunburst finish,
was made in 1997.*

*The Smiths' first album appeared this year,
with Johnny Marr (below) using classic
guitars – including a Strat – for some
gloriously melodic parts.*

CBS sold Fender to the company's management at the very start of the year, and an exciting new era for the firm was about to begin. Fenders were abundant at Live Aid, the famine-relief benefit that grabbed a global audience of one-and-a-half billion people across 170 countries. Edge (above) with U2 was a notable on-stage stylist at the event. Yngwie Malmsteen's debut album was out this year (right), an altogether more explosive and metallic affair.

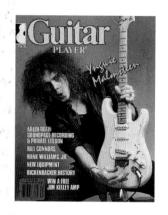

At the end of January 1985, almost exactly 20 years after acquiring it, CBS confirmed that it would sell Fender to ten "employees and foreign distributors," led by Bill Schultz. The contract for the sale was formalized in February and completed in March. The price was $12½ million.

The problems Schultz and his team faced were legion. Probably the most immediate was the fact that the Fullerton factories were not included in the deal, and so US production stopped in February 1985. However, the new team had stockpiled bodies and necks, and had acquired some existing inventory of completed guitars as well as production machinery. The company went from employing some 800 people in early 1984 to just over 100 a year later.

Administration HQ was established in Brea, California, not far from Fullerton (six years later Fender moved admin from Brea to Scottsdale, Arizona), and a search began for a factory site in the general Orange County area of Los Angeles.

Fender had been working on a couple of radical guitars before the sale campaign. One was a John Page design, the Performer. It started life intended for US production, but with nowhere to build it there, manufacturing was started at Fujigen in Japan.

The Performer had a distinctive body shape, twin slanted pickups, 24 frets, and an arrow-shape headstock quite different from the usual Strat derivative. It was based on the 1969 Swinger head, to avoid the need for a new trademark, and was a reaction to the drooped headstock of the newly prevalent "superstrat" guitars popularized by American guitarmaker Charvel–Jackson.

Despite the strengths of the thoroughly modern Performer, the model was destabilized by the turbulence from the sale. It did manage to stay in Fender's list until 1986, but it now seems a pity that such a brave guitar should have been dropped for reasons largely unconnected with the instrument itself.

Of less interest was the Katana, a response to another fashion of the time among guitar makers: the weird body shape. Dealers had pressured Fender for an odd-shape guitar, but players resisted the styling and the imposed Japanese origin of the Katana, and it too limped on only until 1986.

The Japanese operation became Fender's lifeline, providing much-needed product to a company that still had no US factory. Around 80 per cent of the guitars that Fender US sold from late 1984 to mid 1986 were made in Japan. All the guitars in Fender's 1985 catalog were made in Japan, including the new Contemporary Stratocasters and Contemporary Telecasters. These were the first relatively conventional Fenders to feature the increasingly fashionable heavy-duty vibrato systems and string-clamps made popular on superstrats.

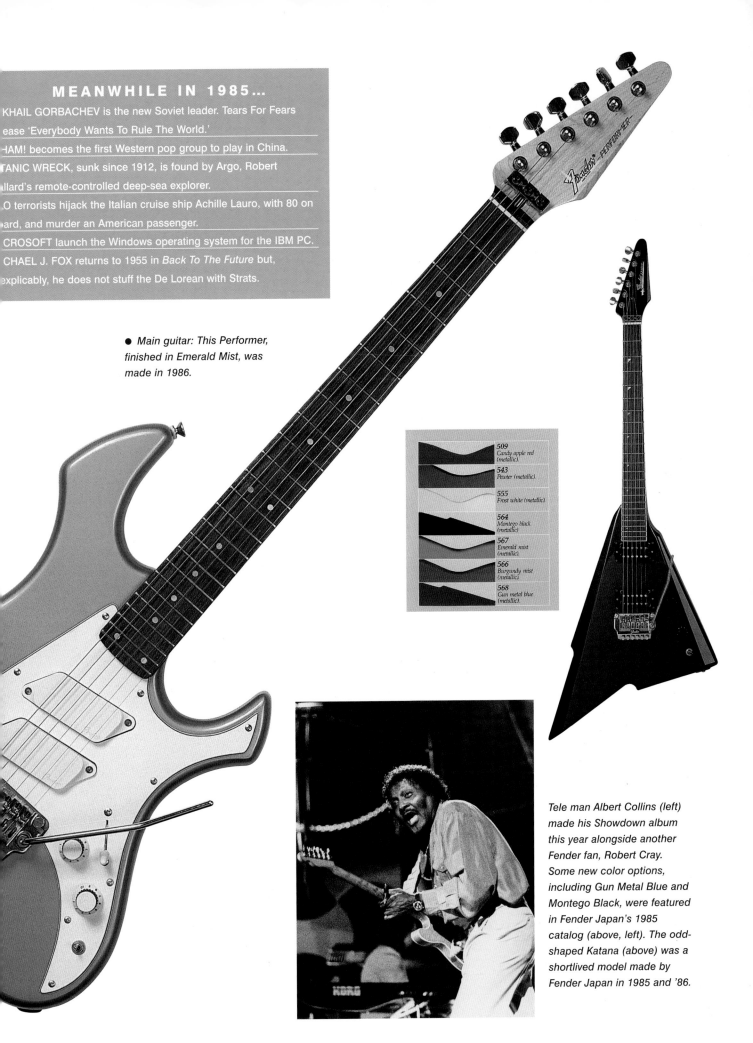

● *Main guitar: This Performer,
finished in Emerald Mist, was
made in 1986.*

509
*Candy apple red
(metallic).*

543
Pewter (metallic).

555
Frost white (metallic).

564
*Montego black
(metallic).*

567
*Emerald mist
(metallic).*

566
*Burgundy mist
(metallic).*

568
*Gun metal blue
(metallic).*

*Tele man Albert Collins (left)
made his Showdown album
this year alongside another
Fender fan, Robert Cray.
Some new color options,
including Gun Metal Blue and
Montego Black, were featured
in Fender Japan's 1985
catalog (above, left). The odd-
shaped Katana (above) was a
shortlived model made by
Fender Japan in 1985 and '86.*

Jerry Donahue
Telecasting

1986
Crafted in Corona

Fender's reputation among musicians was as strong as ever, with hardly a live show escaping some glimpse of the company logo – maybe on an instrument in the hands of the virtuosic Jerry Donahue (above) or Pretenders frontwoman Chrissie Hynde (right). But a plan was under way that would establish playable, high-quality, US-made versions of the classic models: the American Standard series.

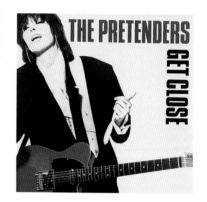

A growing number of models was being manufactured by Fender Japan for worldwide sale, as well as the instruments it made that were only available on the domestic Japanese market. Back in the United States, Fender had finally established a factory, It was at Corona, California, about 20 miles east of the now defunct Fullerton site.

Production had started at Corona on a very limited scale toward the end of 1985. At first the new factory was building only about five guitars per day for the Vintage reissue series.

The new operation had little or no money to invest in fresh tooling for brand new designs, and the team had learned from mistakes like the Elite vibrato that the focus had to be on simplicity. In general, they figured, simplicity makes things work, and does not get in the way of the player.

So it was that electric-guitar boss Dan Smith and his colleagues decided that the most advantageous way forward was to re-establish the US side of Fender's production with a good, basic Stratocaster, Telecaster, Precision Bass, and Jazz Bass. These would involve very little new costs, and would, the company hoped, be seen as a continuation of the very best of Fender's long-standing American traditions.

This general plan translated specifically into the American Standard series. The Stratocaster version was the first model to be launched, in 1986, with the Telecaster, Precision, and Jazz following on two years

later. The American Standard Stratocaster was an efficacious piece of re-interpretation. It drew from the best of the original Stratocaster, but was updated with a 22-fret neck that had a slightly flatter fingerboard, and a revised vibrato unit. The vibrato had twin knife-edge pivot points, which Fender claimed would provide increased stability, a smoother action, and much less opportunity for the number-one enemy of vibrato bridges: friction. The flat saddles, cast in stainless-steel, offered the most obvious visual clue to the presence of the new vibrato, while other technical changes allowed greater arm travel.

A new set of six color options – Arctic White, Black, Brown Sunburst, Gun Metal Blue, Pewter, and Torino Red – was made immediately available for the American Standard Strat, with changes and additions following.

Once the Corona plant's production lines reached full speed, the American Standard Strat proved to be an extremely successful model for the revitalized Fender company. By the early 1990s the guitar would be a best-seller, notching up some 25,000 sales annually. In fact in many markets today, including the United States, the various American Standard models ("Standard" was dropped in 2000 and then reinstated in 2008) remain firmly among the bestselling American-made Fender models.

● *Main guitar: This American
Standard Stratocaster, in
Frost Red, was made in 1991.*

*Blues-rocker Jeff Healey (right)
demonstrated his unusual lap
style on an American Standard
Strat in this 1995 ad. The
Stratocaster was joined by the
American Standard Telecaster in
1988, as seen in the ad pictured
(above, right).*

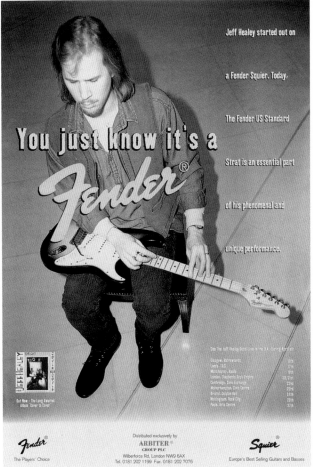

Custom made CA

A new Custom Shop was started this year, at first making one-off artist models but gradually building a much wider role. Fender-toting musicians making waves included Stevie Ray Vaughan, whose *Live Alive* LP (right) featured blistering blues-based rock, while Thurston Moore (above) mixed noise-for-noise-sake and huge riffs to help New York band Sonic Youth turn out *Sister*, one of their finest albums yet.

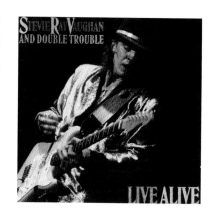

In 1987 the Custom Shop was officially established at the new Corona plant so that Fender could build one-offs and special orders. While this specialist role continued – customers have ranged from Chet Atkins to Eric Johnson (below) to Lou Reed – the Custom Shop would go on to develop a much wider function within Fender's expanding business.

The Shop's activities gradually grew into three main areas. First there are the one-offs, or  Master Built guitars. These are exactly what most people would understand as the work of a custom shop: instruments made by one person with acute attention to detail – and a price to match. The second type is the limited edition, a special numbered run of anything from a handful to several hundred of a specific model. And the third type appeared when the Custom Shop began to produce a general line of catalog models.

In its second year the Custom Shop produced the 40th Anniversary Telecaster, the first limited-edition production run. The limited run of 300 proved too low for the demand, so the Shop's next limited edition – the HLE (Haynes Limited Edition) Stratocaster – was upped to 500 units. Other numbered runs continued to appear from the Custom Shop and became an important part of its job. A logical extension to the limited editions would start in 1992 with the Shop's

first catalog of standard Custom Shop products. No production limit is put on these models other than the confines of the Shop's capacity.

The expansion of the Custom Shop's business prompted a move in 1993 to new buildings (but still close to the Corona factory), to gain extra space and improve efficiency, and a further move during 1998 to Fender's new Corona plant.

An early job for the Custom Shop was to build a yellow Vintage reissue Strat for Jeff Beck. At this stage Beck vetoed Fender's wish to produce a Jeff Beck signature edition Strat, and the design intended for that purpose evolved into the Strat Plus. A Jeff Beck signature Strat not dissimilar to the Plus finally appeared in 1991.

The Strat Plus adopted a roller nut and locking tuners, fashionable features designed to improve vibrato performance. It was also the first Fender with new Lace Sensor pickups. Don Lace, an expert in magnetics, had tried to interest Fender in his designs before the CBS sale, and discussions reopened afterwards.

Fender wanted to continue in the direction it had started with the Elite pickups and was aiming for an ideal that combined low noise with low magnetic attraction, but at the same time still delivering the classic single-coil sound. The result was Lace Sensor pickups.

● *Main guitar: This Strat
Plus, in Graffiti Yellow finish,
was made in 1990.*

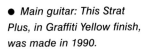

*The Custom Shop was started by John
Page (below left) and John Stevens,
pictured in 1987 with an early job, a Foam
Green Tele Thinline for Elliot Easton of
The Cars. Luthier Fred Stuart is seen at
work at the Shop (above) in 1990.*

*Fender's US amp business was
started afresh at Lake Oswego,
Oregon, in 1986 under Bill
Hughes. Two of the new tube
models included The Twin and
Dual Showman, seen in this
1987 flyer (right).*

1988

Sign here please, Eric

Eric Clapton became the first musician honored with a Fender signature-edition production guitar. He was closely followed by Yngwie Malmsteen, and in the coming years many more guitarists and bassists would be similarly celebrated (signature catalog, right). Meanwhile, moves were made to produce guitars further afield, with some of Fender's Squier-brand instruments now coming from Korea and, briefly, India.

The first signature guitar produced by Fender was the Eric Clapton Stratocaster. In fact, the first musician with whom Fender informally discussed the possibility of a signature model had been James Burton, back in 1981, but Burton had to wait until 1990 for his signature Telecaster to appear.

Signature models have become important to the Fender line in the years since, but at first this was another bonus brought about by the new Custom Shop, which was actively pushing to pro players its services for building one-off instruments that could be tailored to individual requirements.

Clapton asked Fender to make him a guitar that had the distinct V-shape neck of his favorite 1930s Martin acoustic guitar, as well as what he described as a "compressed" pickup sound. Various prototypes were built for Clapton by George Blanda at the Custom Shop, and the final design eventually went on sale to the public in 1988.

Fender demonstrated to Clapton that Lace Sensor pickups and a midrange-boosting active circuit could deliver the sound he was after, and curiously the production model even offers a blocked-off vintage-style vibrato unit, carefully duplicating that feature of Clapton's fave Strat (he never used vibrato, but disliked the sound of hardtail non-vibrato Strats). Clapton had retired his faithful old "bitser" Strat, Blackie, in 1987, and started to play his new signature models soon after.

Also released in 1988 was the second signature model, the Yngwie Malmsteen Stratocaster. The most unusual aspect of the Swedish metal guitarist's instrument was the scalloped fingerboard. Malmsteen claims that the absence of physical contact with the fingerboard enables him to play even faster than his already lightning technique allows.

A good number of Fender signature models would follow these first two. Some were made in the Custom Shop; others came from the main factories or further afield. Each one generally bore features favored by the named artist. The company chooses its signature-model players for their contributions as musicians and their continuing involvement with Fender. "It's really more of a tribute rather than anybody getting rich," Fender's Dan Smith once explained. "The players are compensated fairly, and everybody gets the same royalty."

This year, three more American Standard models – Tele, the Jazz Bass, and Precision – joined the earlier Strat. The Tele was updated with a 22-fret neck and a six-saddle bridge. And the newest model from Fender Japan was the Strat XII (pictured opposite), only the second solid electric 12-string produced by Fender.

● *Main guitar: This Eric
Clapton Stratocaster, in Torino
Red, was made in 1990.*

*More vintage-like models
came from the US (catalog,
opposite, top left) and Japan,
which also made this Blue
Flower Strat (far right) as well
as the Strat XII (right).
Signature models kicked off
this year with the Clapton
Strat (promo material, below).*

**U.S. SIGNATURE
SERIES**

1989
Superduperstrat

The first full-blown attempt by Fender to adopt the superstrat style of guitar, which had become so popular in the 1980s, arrived in the shape of the HM series, out this year and made in America. Later HM models, also shortlived, included Japanese-built instruments (catalog, above, and a very unusual Fender logo, right, on that "pointy" headstock). Also in Japan, Heartfield – a new experimental Fender-related brand – was introduced.

As the 1980s drew to a close, Fender was keeping an eye carefully trained on the continuing popularity of so-called superstrat guitars. These had been developed by Charvel/Jackson, manufacturing in the US and then Japan. Subsequently, many brands such as Washburn, Ibanez, Kramer, and others adopted elements of the design in various forms.

The superstrat had started by considering a classic Stratocaster as its basis, squaring the body sides, stretching the horns, making the contouring bolder, and slimming the overall shape. The revamped body carried powerful combinations of single-coil and humbucker pickups, evolving to the preferred combination of two single-coils plus bridge humbucker. All this was partnered by a double-locking heavy-duty fine-tunable vibrato system, meant for extreme pitch shifting. Access to the highest of the 24 frets was improved with a through-neck and deeper cutaways, and the design also popularized the drooped "pointy" headstock. Fender's first nod toward this style had been with 1985's Performer, but this had effectively been lost in the difficulties surrounding the sale of Fender by CBS. The HM Stratocaster series, begun in 1989, tried again. This time the "HM" name was a big clue: metal guitarists were the major players of such guitars, though more mainstream guitarists such as Jeff Beck (1989 *Guitar Shop* album, opposite) had been briefly seduced.

Fender's HM Strats started out US-made, with most of the expected superstrat features on board,

including a locking vibrato, and came with three different pickup configurations: two single-coils and a bridge humbucker; one Lace Sensor and a bridge humbucker; or two humbuckers. All were shortlived: it seemed that players generally still expected traditional Fenders from Fender.

Meanwhile the US Contemporary Stratocaster, also new in 1989, put the locking vibrato system and single/single/humbucker line-up on a conventional Strat body and neck, but this too did not last long.

A few years later Fender tried again unsuccessfully, with Japanese-made HMs (see catalog, top of page), although it wasn't really until the Floyd Rose Classic Stratocaster of 1992 that the company hit upon a reasonably successful blend of traditional and new features.

Perhaps a way to avoid the un-Fender Fenders problem was to use a completely different brandname? Squier had become closely associated with Fender, so the Heartfield brand was concocted for a line of guitars considered too radical to be Fenders. They were designed by Fender US and Fender Japan and built at Fujigen in Japan. Some did have "Heartfield by Fender" logos, in a similar way to Squier, but the experiment was halted by 1993.

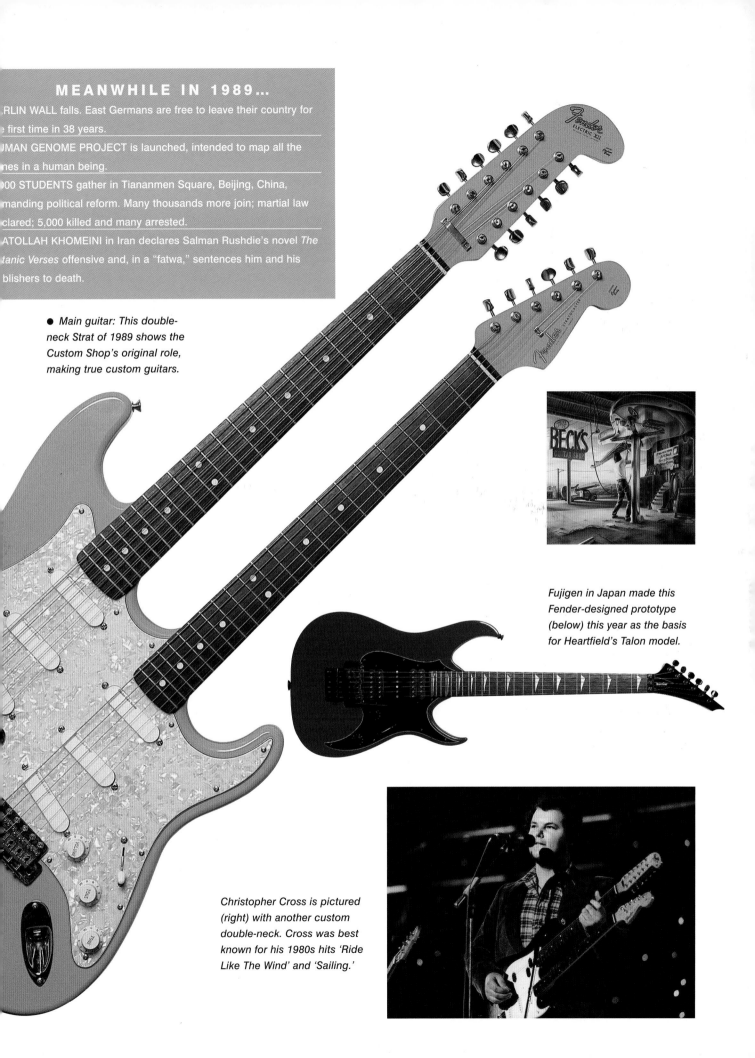

● *Main guitar: This double-neck Strat of 1989 shows the Custom Shop's original role, making true custom guitars.*

Fujigen in Japan made this Fender-designed prototype (below) this year as the basis for Heartfield's Talon model.

Christopher Cross is pictured (right) with another custom double-neck. Cross was best known for his 1980s hits 'Ride Like The Wind' and 'Sailing.'

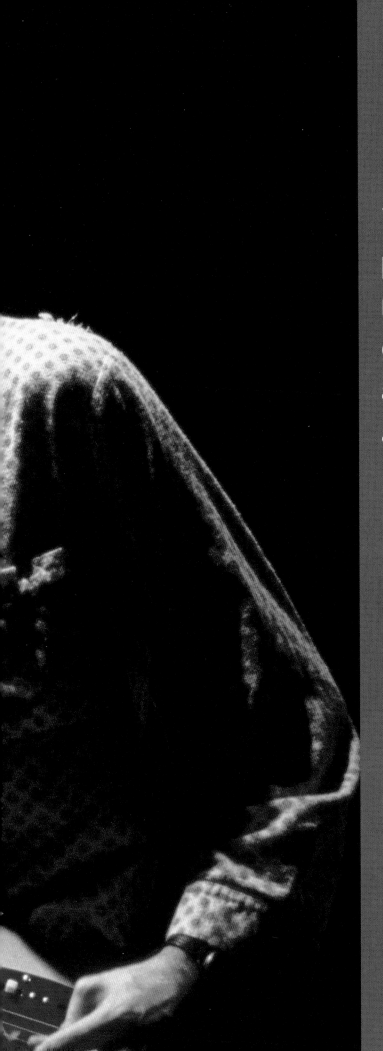

"Fender was perfectly placed for the 1990s retro craze, with its glittering past continually available for re-evaluation and re-engineering."

90s

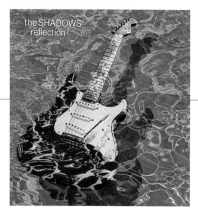

the SHADOWS reflection

Albert, Danny, James

Plenty of activity this year, with new five-string bass guitars, a trio of signature models, and a reissue amp series that kicked off gloriously with a '59 tweed Bassman. But in a hallowed saleroom in London, another kind of history was made when a Stratocaster (pictured on the catalog, right) apparently played by Hendrix at Woodstock was sold for a record price of $270,000. Treating your own guitar like the Strat on this Shadows album (above) would probably void the warranty.

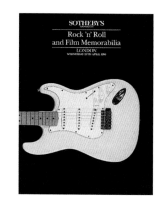

SOTHEBY'S
Rock 'n' Roll
and Film Memorabilia
LONDON
WEDNESDAY 25TH APRIL, 1990

More signature model guitars appeared this year as Fender became increasingly aware of the promotional value of such instruments and "branding" was everywhere as the hip new marketing philosophy. All three of these new-for-1990 signature instruments were Telecasters.

Classic Texas bluesman Albert Collins was honored with a model that exchanged the neck pickup for a humbucker. Explosive technician Danny Gatton got a signature Tele with two "blade" pickups, a modified bridge, and body decoration. And former Presley sideman James Burton's model had three Strat-layout single-coils – with some bodies finished in a paisley pattern much more lurid than the guitarist's original Red Paisley Tele.

The reissue program had gone so well for guitars and basses that Fender decided to do the same for its amplifiers. The amp department had just introduced (at last!) a good new solid-state line – the M-80, the Rad, the Hot, and the Jam – which had proved especially successful with younger players. Now Fender felt confident enough to delve back into the past to provide inspiration at the top of its pricelist.

The first reissue amp, out in 1990, was an obvious choice: a tweed '59 Bassman. This was almost certainly Fender's most famous amp and, despite the name, it was a guitarist's dream. Real vintage examples had become increasingly hard to find, let alone the expense involved when one did surface. A handful of other

reissues has followed, such as the "blackface" '65 Twin Reverb, and very popular they have proved.

During the 1980s a number of musicians and small bass-makers had developed the five-string bass guitar, with a low string tuned to B, and – unlike Fender's peculiar high-C Bass V – retaining the relatively wide string-spacing of a regular bass. The modern five-string bass had become an essential addition to the instruments carried by many touring and recording bassists across many styles, and by the end of the 1980s a five-string model appeared on most bass-maker's pricelists. Fender waited until 1990 to introduce its first five-string bass models. These were the Jazz Plus V (pictured, left) and the HM V. The Jazz Plus was an active-circuit Jazz Bass; the HM a three-pickup, slab-bodied heavy-rock machine.

Aside from the shortlived Esprit and Flame guitars of 1984, Fender had not strayed much from its customary bolt-on neck. But three new Set Neck Teles, designed this year, would soon offer Fender fans a glued joint, enabling the smooth, heel-less junction where the neck meets the body, which some guitarists find more playable.

● *Main guitar: This James
Burton Telecaster, finished in
Black With Gold Paisley, was
made in 1991.*

*Danny Gatton (above) poses with his
original customized Tele, the guitar that
inspired this year's Fender signature
model. The Jazz Plus V (left) was one of
the first Fender five-string basses. The
catalog close-up (below) shows Burton
with a his Frost Red signature model.*

The James Burton model
"As much a James loved those stock Telecasters
he used with Ricky and Elvis, they didn't give him
all the sounds he wanted. So we installed three
Fender-Lace® Sensors and added a five-position
switch. The middle sensor sits low so as not to
obstruct his picking. Now he gets those Strat
sounds that you can't get from a Tele. The neck
still has that same vintage feel and headstock
cut, so that he can bend strings behind the nut."
George Blanda

1991
Down Mexico way

A new Fender factory based just over the California border in Mexico had been making amplifiers and cabinets for a few years, but during 1991 its first guitar products became evident, including the Standard Strat, Tele, P-Bass and Jazz. More signature models were built at the US factory, for Robert Cray (above) and Jeff Beck, while another superstrat-style instrument came along, known as the Prodigy.

Fender US came up with a new design in 1991 called the Prodigy, another shortlived attempt to compete with superstrats and their progeny. The Prodigy had an offset-waist body with sharper horns than a Stratocaster, the requisite two single-coils and a humbucker, and an optional locking vibrato. There was a matching bass, too.

Significantly, the Prodigy was among the first Fender guitars to receive attention at the company's new factory in Ensenada, Mexico, which had been established in 1987. Ensenada is some 180 miles south of Los Angeles and is situated just across the California/Mexico border. Fender amps started to appear from Mexico in 1989, with guitars following soon after. The factory would be entirely rebuilt in 1994 after a disastrous fire.

By early 1992 the Mexican factory was assembling around 175 Fender Standard Stratocasters per day, and by 1995 had a capacity for producing 600 instruments a day. Bodies and necks for the Made In Mexico guitars were produced at the US factory in Corona and sent down to the Mexican plant. There they were sanded, painted, buffed, and assembled with Mexican-made hardware and pickups. The factory also produced all Fender's strings.

By late 1997, Mexico would be assembling around 150,000 Fender guitars a year, compared to some 85,000 at Corona, with a workforce of around 1,000 at the Mexico factory and 700 at Corona.

The chief advantage to Fender of its Mexican and some offshore production sites is the cheapness of the labor. Fender has like many Western companies searched far and wide for this expediency. In addition to continuing products from Korea, the lowest-price Squier-brand Fender guitars were by 1999 being made at two factories in China, a source the company had used since the start of the 1990s.

New models from the US factory included two signature Jeff Beck and Robert Cray Strats. Set Neck Teles were launched, with a Country Artist (pictured opposite) added in 1992.

An Associated Press wire report for 21st March marked a sad occasion: "Clarence Leo Fender, whose revolutionary Stratocaster was the guitar of choice for rock stars from Buddy Holly to Jimi Hendrix, died today. He was 82. Fender was found unconscious in his Fullerton home by his wife, Phyllis, and died on the way to hospital. Fender had suffered Parkinson's disease for decades but continued to work on guitar designs." Leo had been at his bench at his G&L company just the day before, tinkering with yet another guitar improvement.

● *Main guitar: This Prodigy II,
in Lake Placid Blue finish, was
made in 1991.*

*J. Mascis and his finely decorated
Jazzmaster (right) were at the heart of
Dinosaur Jr.'s excellent Green Mind
album, out this year. The Set Neck Tele
Country Artist (below, top) came out in
1992, while the Custom Shop made
100 of this James Jamerson Tribute
Bass (bottom) in collaboration with
The Bass Centre store in Los Angeles.*

S.R.V.(slight return)

Fender Japan added a 70s Precision and a '75 Jazz Bass reissue to a Vintage line that still leaned heavily on Strats and Teles (ad, above), and the US factory contributed two more old-style Strats, a '54 and a '60. The signature series was expanding too, resulting in this impressive ad (right) that was also made available as a handy spot-the-Fender-man poster. Bon Jovi's Richie Sambora was there, although his signature model didn't actually go on sale until 1993.

Fender's new US-made "hot" Texas Special Strat-type single-coils first appeared on this year's new Stevie Ray Vaughan signature Strat. The model had been agreed before Vaughan's tragic death in 1990 in a helicopter accident, when the guitarist's career was at full blast.

The signature model was based on Vaughan's well-used Stratocaster known as "Number One" which consisted of a basic 1959 instrument modified with a 1962 neck. Fender's Stevie Ray Vaughan Stratocaster duplicated the original instrument's substantial SRV logo on the pickguard, and also featured an unusual left-handed vibrato system, as favored by the Texas guitarist... whose work had often revealed a strong stylistic link with left-hander Jimi Hendrix.

More signature models appeared: two for Telecaster supremo Jerry Donahue – one version made in the US, the other in Japan – and for bassist Stu Hamm, who had worked with guitar virtuosi Steve Vai and Joe Satriani. Hamm's bass was the Urge, a clever blend of Jazz and Precision features that created a multi-pickup bass with wide tonal potential.

Floyd Rose, a guitar-hardware designer known for his heavy-duty locking vibrato system, joined forces with Fender late in 1991 when Fender acquired exclusive rights to Floyd Rose products. Other makers could still buy licensed hardware, but Fender seemed more interested in access to Rose's design skills, as well as the assistance that his name brought in selling guitars to the heavy metal market. To such musicians

"Floyd Rose" was almost synonymous with the heavy-duty double-locking vibrato systems so closely associated with the intense, highly-technical style of playing that peaked in the early 1990s. Fender's Floyd Rose Classic Stratocaster was launched in 1992.

The Custom Shop's "catalog" items expanded with the introduction of the American Classic Stratocaster, effectively an upscale Shop version of the factory's best-selling American Standard Strat. Several items were added to the American Classic line in coming years, including Jazz Basses and Telecasters. More unusual was the Shop's Bajo Sexto, a baritone Telecaster with a long 30-inch scale and a resulting deep, twangy tone.

Further from home, Korea was a new Fender production source, providing the Squier Series Strat and Tele, each with regular Fender logo and small "Squier Series" on the headstock.

A year after Mike Lewis had moved to head up the amplifier marketing department, Fender's amp series was gradually remodeled into a uniform style, dumping the old "red-knob" look of recent years for something approaching classic Fender visuals. Introductions this year included the solid-state 25-watt BXR, 65-watt Deluxe 112, and 16-watt Stage 112, the hybrid 25-watt Champ 25, and the tube 60-watt Concert and 60-watt Super Amp.

● *Main guitar: This Stevie Ray Vaughan Stratocaster, in Sunburst, was made in 1992.*

PEARL JAM

John Frusciante (above) departed the Red Hot Chilli Peppers this year; Stu Hamm's signature bass was the Urge (below); and Pearl Jam's debut Ten (left) featured Mike McCready's Strat and Stone Gossard's Jag.

Hi-ho Harley

The amp Custom Shop offered the high-end, vintage-flavored Vibro-King and Tone-Master as its first products, while the existing guitar Custom Shop reflected on a 90th Anniversary Harley-Davidson Strat. Comings and goings among Fender players included a debut from Liz Phair (opposite) and the death at 61 of the great Texas bluesman Albert Collins (memorial ad, right). G-Vox (above) was Fender's ill-fated computer guitar-teaching system.

With the continuing success of the guitar Custom Shop, this year saw the start at Scottsdale, Arizona, of an amp equivalent, with ex-Matchless electronics expert Bruce Zinky in charge. The intention was to make limited quantities of expensive, high-quality products. The amp Shop would not build far-out made-to-order items, but generally would follow the guitar outfit's increasingly important business in defining a catalog of regular items.

Artists could collaborate on individually crafted items, but broadly speaking the hand-built line would be drawn from reinterpretations of Fender's classic tube amps of the 1940s, 50s and early 60s. The first models to appear from the amp Custom Shop were the Vibro-King 60-watt 3x10 combo and the Tone-Master 100-watt piggyback amp, with a choice of 2x12 or 4x12 cabinet, all finished in cream Tolex. In the meantime at the guitar Custom Shop, over in Corona, a link was being forged with motorcycle manufacturer Harley-Davidson.

The result was the Fender Harley-Davidson 90th Anniversary Commemorative Stratocaster in a very limited run of 109 pieces. The stunning hand-engraved aluminum body summoned up the shiny exterior of a Harley, while the bird's-eye maple neck and ebony fingerboard would please anyone who actually got to play one of these creations.

The signature-guitar list continued to grow, this year with the addition of two new models, for Clarence White and Richie Sambora. The Clarence White Telecaster was named for the brilliant Byrds and Kentucky Colonels guitarist, tragically killed by a drunk driver in 1973. The White Tele was fitted with his favored Scruggs banjo-style detuners for first and sixth strings, and the B-bender string-pull device that he developed with Byrds drummer Gene Parsons.

Bon Jovi's Richie Sambora helped devise a Strat to respond to his fiery playing, with Floyd Rose double-locking vibrato, a DiMarzio bridge humbucker plus Texas Special single-coils, and a flatter, wider fingerboard. A personal touch came with the inlaid stars for position markers.

On a cultural note, the Fullerton Museum Center – not far from the site of Leo Fender's original workshops – exhibited *Five Decades Of Fender,* organized by guitar historian Richard Smith. Included were instruments and an array of special memorabilia from Fender as well as Music Man and G&L. Remarkably, this was the very first exhibition to feature Fender's achievements. "Leo forever changed the course of popular music," is how Smith admirably summed it up.

● *Main guitar: This Harley-Davidson 90th Anniversary Commemorative Stratocaster was made in 1993.*

The Clarence White Telecaster (right) was out, with two rear-mounted Scruggs detuners and a B-string pull device for country bends. A limited Custom Shop model was the delightful Playboy Strat (ad, below), and Liz Phair (with Duo-Sonic, above) released her acclaimed folk-grunge debut album this year.

The Choice of
Every Generation

Fender Guitar and
Bass Amplifiers

ELECTRONICS

**Fulfil your
fantasies.**

Custom Shop

Dreams-Come-True

The Stratocaster turned a mature, sprightly 40 this year, and to mark the occasion Fender issued a stylish 40th Anniversary model, suitably produced in a special limited-edition run of exactly 1,954 instruments. The vintage reissue business was still as busy as ever, underlined in an ad where musicians were invited to travel through time (right), while the Custom Shop offered instruments as fanciful as the customer's imagination would allow (catalog cover, above).

The Custom Shop was finding more and more of its guitar business was drawn from the regularly produced catalog items it offered. However, starting in 1994 there was a renewed emphasis on one-off productions, and a fresh indulgence of the whims of the select band of Master Builders – the ten or so top luthiers working at the Shop.

The Custom Shop's art guitars are highly decorated instruments – though "objects" might be a better description as it's doubtful that many end up gigged in a sweaty club. More likely they're put on display, much like a piece of sculpture. One of the reasons the Master Builders were encouraged to develop these ultra-fancy pieces was for traveling Fender "art" shows touring the US and Europe, promoting the Custom Shop's capabilities when time and money are not limitations.

In this first year, the art guitars included Master Builder Fred Stuart's Egyptian Telecaster, with pyramids and snakes and runes hand-carved by George Amicay in a finish of Corian synthetic stone. There was also the Aloha Strat, for which Master Builder J.T. English had been inspired by Hawaiian art, 1930s resonator guitars, and Art Deco. Ron Chacy engraved the aluminum body, which was colored by Peter Kellett using selective anodizing. A "plain" aluminum Aloha would become a limited-edition 1995 model dedicated to the memory of the great Fender designer and engineer Freddie Tavares. The necessarily extended period of production of the art guitars made them very expensive. The Shop

apparently turned down $75,000 for an "Aztec-Mayan" Tele, while a "Regina del Mare" Strat built in 1997 for Fender's first Catalina Island Blues Festival was sold at a music charity auction for $50,000.

Unusually, the Corona factory rather than the Custom Shop produced a numbered limited edition this year, the 40th Anniversary 1954 Stratocaster (although there was a 40-only run of a Custom Shop Concert Edition). Exactly 1,954 of the factory 40th Strat were made. And American Standard Strats gained a small 40th Anniversary headstock medallion to mark this special year.

Signature models launched included the Dick Dale Strat, recreating the surf king's guitar, the one that he affectionately referred to as The Beast. Jazz-blues stylist Robben Ford had reinterpreted the shortlived 1980s Esprit Ultra as the basis for his special signature models, started back in 1989 with some Japan-made instruments. However, from this year the Custom Shop took over production (see the Ford Ultra model, pictured opposite).

● *Main guitar: This Custom Shop "art guitar" was the third Regina Del Mare Strat, made in 1998, for Fender's regular Catalina Island Blues Festival.*

Blur's Parklife album (below, left) was out, with Graham Coxon (below) often opting for a Tele. Strats, meanwhile, were still haunted by Jimi's ghost (ad, above), and a new signature model was the Robben Ford Ultra SP (right).

Bash 'em up a bit

Joining the elite club of signature-model endorsers were Bonnie Raitt (see opposite), Roscoe Beck, Buddy Guy (with polka-dot Strat, opposite), and Waylon Jennings. More Foto Flame models appeared, looking as if they were made from expensive figured wood thanks to a clever photo-printing technique. And the Relic series was announced, bringing the appeal of aged vintage guitars to new instruments.

Some artists had been asking the Custom Shop to make them a replica of a favorite old guitar or two, usually because the original was much too valuable and cherished to risk taking on the road. But then Keith Richards told the Shop that some replicas made for him for a Stones tour looked too new. "Bash 'em up a bit and I'll play 'em," suggested Richards.

So the Shop began to include wear-and-tear distress marks to replicate the overall look of a battered old original (guitar, that is, not Mr. Richards). Then J.W. Black, a Master Builder at the Custom Shop, came up with the idea of offering these aged replica guitars as regular catalog items, and naming them Relics.

The Shop made two aged 1950s-era samples: a Nocaster (the in-between Broadcaster/Telecaster with no model name) and a "Mary Kaye" Strat (blond body, gold-plated hardware), and announced the new Relic scheme in 1995. Soon the Custom Shop was reacting to the demand generated from these samples by offering a line of three Relic Strats and a Relic Nocaster. The Relics would prove a remarkable success, with the Mary Kaye version becoming the Shop's single best-selling model of the late 1990s.

The line would be expanded from 1998 by offering three types of "re-creations" in what would become known as the Time Machine series. First are the N.O.S. (New Old Stock) guitars, intended as pristine replicas that are produced as closely as possible to original brand-new instruments that would have come off the

Fender production line during the period at large. Next are the Closet Classics, which are meant to be like guitars bought new years ago, played a little bit… and then shoved under the bed or in a closet. Third is the Relic style, as already mentioned, with "aged" dings and wear added by the Shop.

By 2000 the Custom Shop's Time Machine series would include a '64 Jazz Bass, '51 Nocaster, '59 Precision Bass, '56, '60, and '69 Stratocasters, and a '63 Telecaster – each available in the three different levels of aging, and all listing in the US at around the $2,500 to $3,000 mark. These guitars obviously appeal to a relatively small but growing number of Fender fans who were keen to acquire a new guitar that had the feel and sound of an oldie and – in the case of the Relics – was made to look as if decades of wear-and-tear have stained the fingerboard, scuffed the body, and tarnished the hardware. The Time Machine series is a brilliant move, the nearest Fender has come with new instruments to the almost indefinable appeal of vintage guitars, which many thought was firmly and safely locked away in the past.

Also this year, Fender bought the hollowbody guitar maker Guild, gradually rationalizing the lines with an accent on traditional design.

● *Main guitar: This Relic 60s Stratocaster, in Daphne Blue, was made in 1998.*

Fender recreated its classic ads (below) with the famous "You won't part with yours" tag. The first woman with a signature Fender was Bonnie Raitt (below); this one (right) was made in 1999. Buddy Guy (above) was another musican with a new signature Strat this year, although the polka-dot version would have to wait a few years.

Left-hander Kurt Cobain with his favored live guitar (below), a Mustang with added humbucker. He merged this with a Jaguar to come up with his unusual Jag-Stang.

● *Main guitar: This left-hand Jag-Stang, in Fiesta Red, was made in 1997.*

The Lone Star Strat (below; and catalog, right) was like an American Standard with hot pickups, including a Seymour Duncan bridge humbucker.

1996
Jag-shaped Stang

The Fender company was 50 years old this year, and a number of celebratory models and promotions marked the occasion (see the ad and anniversary decal, above). Player models included a posthumous hybrid guitar for Kurt Cobain, various Ventures guitars and basses, and Richie Sambora's Japanese black-paisley Strat (left). The hot-pickup Tex Mex Strat, suitably produced at the Mexican factory, was endorsed by Jimmie Vaughan – and became Vaughan's signature model in '97.

Fenders beyond the ubiquitous Strats and Teles were proving popular with so-called grunge guitarists: Seattle supremo Kurt Cobain of Nirvana had played Jaguars and Mustangs; Steve Turner in Mudhoney opted for a Mustang; J. Mascis of Dinosaur Jr. was often seen with his Jazzmaster. And the reason was relatively straightforward. These guitars had the comforting Fender logo on the head but could be bought more cheaply secondhand than Strats or Teles. The ethics suited grunge perfectly.

Back in 1993, Cobain decided to take cut-up photos of his Jag and Mustang and stick them together, this way and that, trying combinations to see what they would look like. Larry Brooks of the Custom Shop took Cobain's paste-ups, assembled the design, and added a contour or two to improve balance and feel.

After Cobain's untimely death in 1994, his family collaborated with Fender to release a Japanese-made production version of the instrument, named the Fender Jag-Stang. Cobain's guitar hit the market in 1996.

The Lone Star Stratocaster, also launched in 1996, was one example of how the Fender R&D department worked. What it called the core products were taken and subtly (and not-so-subtly) modified to create "new" models based on players' changing tastes. Thus the Lone Star (renamed the American Fat Strat Texas Special in 2000) took an American Standard Strat and changed the pickup configuration to a Seymour Duncan Pearly Gates Plus humbucker at the bridge, plus two of Fender's "hot" Texas Special single-coils.

Fender marked its 50th anniversary this year. In 1946 Leo Fender had parted company with his original partner, Doc Kauffman. Leo dissolved their K&F company and called his new operation Fender Manufacturing (and then renamed it the Fender Electric Instrument Co in December 1947). Fender celebrated "50 Years of Excellence" in 1996 with some factory-made limited-edition anniversary models – the apparently timeless quartet of Telecaster, Precision Bass, Stratocaster, and Jazz Bass – with a special commemorative neckplate. Fender also attached a 50th Anniversary decal (see top of page) to many of the general products sold this year.

The Custom Shop made some anniversary models, too, including 50 of the Pine Telecaster & Amp set (opposite, center). The guitar recreated the original solidbody prototype with its steel-like headstock shape and angled control plate, while the amp was a replica of an early Model 26, with wooden-handled cabinet and chrome strips over a red felt grille.

1997
If left was right...

Courtney Love saw her Custom Shop Venus model (above) become a Squier production item (far left). Fender went Hendrix crazy with back-to-front and hand-painted Jimi Stratocasters. Also on the loose was a fresh outbreak of Fender merchandizing (catalog, right) bringing logo'd hats, shirts, and jackets – but, curiously, no Courtney-style outfits.

Almost exactly 30 years since Jimi Hendrix's career had got underway with his debut album, Fender launched a couple of Hendrix-related US-made Strats, from the Custom Shop and the factory.

Corona's contribution was the simply named Jimi Hendrix Stratocaster. The thinking behind the model was anything but simple. Fender had the go-ahead to make an official model in tribute to Hendrix, the best-known Strat player ever. But Jimi was a left-hander and, despite at least ten per cent of us sharing his cackhandedness, the majority of potential customers for such a guitar would want a right-handed machine.

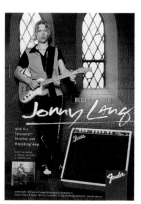

Hendrix would take a normal right-handed Strat, turn it upside down, and re-string it – all in order to accommodate his left-handedness. So Fender decided to make a completely reversed version of one of Jimi's typical late-1960s Strats. The result is pictured opposite. Right-handed players should consider this as a "normal" left-handed guitar that has been turned upside down and re-strung, thus recreating Jimi's experience in reverse, as it were. As if this was not befuddling enough, Fender added a final flourish, no doubt listening to one of Jimi's great backwards-guitar solos as they did. So that the adoring owner could pose to full effect with the new acquisition in front of the mirror, the normal headstock logo was applied completely in reverse. In the mirror, you are Jimi. Now all you have to do is master 'Little Wing.'

The Custom Shop's Jimi Hendrix Monterey Strat was more specific. It recreated the hand-painted Strat that Jimi played at the June 1967 Monterey Pop festival … the one that he famously burned on-stage. Careful examination of pictures taken at the show, pre-conflagration, enabled artist Pamelina Hovnatanian to reconstruct Hendrix's flowery painting for the limited edition of 210 guitars.

Fender's other new signature models included one more Hendrix hint: a Jazz Bass for bassman Noel Redding. Hank Marvin and Jimmie Vaughan had Mexican-made Strats, country legend Merle Haggard a Custom Shop Tuff Dog Tele. Guitar combo The Hellecasters had three signatures: Will Ray's Jazz-a-caster, John Jorgensen's Hellecaster, and Jerry Donahue's restrained Strat.

Pickup fiddling continued: the Big Apple was a two-humbucker Strat with single-coil scratch to humbucker raunch (it was renamed the American Double Fat Strat in 2000); the Roadhouse Strat featured three hot Texas Special single-coils (and was renamed the American Strat Texas Special in 2000); and the California series added Tex Mex pickups to US Strats, Teles and P-Basses.

● *Main guitar: This Jimi Hendrix Stratocaster, in Olympic White finish, was made in 1997.*

From behind a pile of sartorial memorabilia (above), Jimi smiles at the plight of the right-handed guitarist. This limited edition Hendrix Monterey Strat (right) and the Japan-made signature Ritchie Blackmore Strat (ad, top) first appeared this year.

Alongside the Venus were two more new Squier guitars, the Super-Sonic here and the Jagmaster, which was prompted by Bush vocalist Gavin Rossdale's humbucker'd Jazzmaster.

At the end of the 1990s, many guitar-makers were busily looking back to the past for fresh inspiration, and the craze for retro flavors was everywhere. Even the recent Hot Rod Deville and Deluxe amplifiers were now attired in new tweed cloth (ad, above). Buck Owens twanged a sparkle signature Telecaster (right), and three autographed four-strings appeared: the shortlived Duck Dunn and the Geddy Lee P-Basses, plus the Marcus Miller Jazz Bass. All this, and a new US factory too.

Some models were re-organized into new series, with high-end US models grouped as American Deluxes, and reissues together as American Vintages. Retro fever led to the new Toronado and Cyclone (left); upscale, the carved-top Showmasters were Fender's super-est superstrats yet. Fender had recently acquired the De Armond company, famous for old pickups and effects, and began to apply the brand to less expensive Guild-like models from Korea and Indonesia. Fender had owned Guild since 1995.

Biggest event of the year, though, was the opening of a new factory in November, still in Corona, California. The company proudly described the impressive state-of-the-art plant as the world's most expensive and automated. Since starting production at the original Corona factory back in 1985, Fender had grown to occupy a total of 115,000 square feet of space in ten buildings across the city. Such a rambling spread proved increasingly inefficient, and Fender began to plan a new centralized factory during the early 1990s. The new $20 million 177,000-square-feet plant afforded a growing production capacity for the future, and the factory, with a staff of 600, also saw

Fender's long-standing tussle with California's stringent environmental laws at an end, as the new purpose-built paint section was specifically designed to operate without toxic emissions.

Some non-American readers may be confused by references to Fender's "Baja California" factory. This is not the US factory but the Mexican plant which, as we've seen, was established at the end of the 1980s at Ensenada – in an area of Mexico just across the US border known as Baja California.

As the Fender US company neared the 21st century it was using two main sources for Fender-brand instruments: the new Corona factory, and the Mexican plant. Fender Japan's role was dramatically changed, with its continuing high-quality and substantial line almost entirely reserved for sale within Japan, and only a tiny handful of models exported. Fender's move back to be an American manufacturer was – for Fender-brand guitars – virtually complete. Fender's new Corona, California, factory may be some 20 miles from Fullerton and the site of Leo Fender's original workshops, but it's a universe away from the humble steel shacks that were Fender's first home. Leo loved few things more than gadgets and would have been enthralled by the new plant – not least its automated conveyors that supply a vast inventory of guitar components.

● *Main guitar: This Toronado,
finished in Candy Apple Red,
was made in 1998.*

*Fender Japan began to sell almost
exclusively to its home market,
continuing with a large and
impressive line that included models
such as this Bigsby-equipped
Telecaster (below).*

*Ex-Miles Davis bassman Marcus
Miller had a new signature model
based on his own Jazz Bass (left).*

AMERICAN VINTAGE Series
'62 JAZZMASTER & '62 JAGUAR

Past masters

At the close of the 1990s, Fender US used its new California factory and existing Mexican plant as the major sources for Fender-brand instruments, with US-made Jazzmasters and Jaguars (above) appearing for the first time in 20 years or so. Fender Japan, too, continued to make these and many other models, but now most of its products were sold only in Japan – including small-scale guitars (catalog page, right).

This was a year of consolidation for Fender after the opening of its new much-expanded factory in Corona at the end of last year. The company also allowed itself – along with most of the rest of the world – to reflect on some past achievements.

A series of ads had started with the tag-line "The Sound That Creates Legends," stressing once again the fact that an impressive line-up of illustrious names had used and were using Fender instruments. (Some examples from the series are illustrated opposite, plus Jaco Pastorius, left.) The Custom Shop reorganized its successful Relics line, the new guitars and basses with which Fender had managed to get closer to the magical appeal of vintage instruments than ever before. Now there were three strands to the series: the original Relic style, given "aged" knocks and wear as if they had been out on the road for a generation or so; the Closet Classic, made to look as if it had been bought new way back when, played a few times, and then stuck in a closet; and N.O.S. (meaning "New Old Stock") which was intended to seem as if an instrument had been bought brand new in the 1950s or 1960s and then put straight into a time machine which transported it to the present

day. The kind of thing, in fact, that vintage guitar collectors and dealers regularly fantasize about, but which in real life very rarely happens. Especially the time machine part.

Not only this, but the company had discovered another way of mixing the past with the future. The Fender Museum of Music and The Arts Foundation saw its first full year of operation in 1999, although the doors had actually opened the previous summer. The museum's Executive Director was John Page, who had moved across to the new project from his job as head of the Custom Shop.

At first the public evidence of the new scheme was a small preview museum, based in Corona, but Fender expected to expand this over the coming years. The general aim was to create an impressive museum of the performing arts, and in particular to highlight what Page described as "Fender's monumental contribution to the world of modern music." This was intended to take the form of exhibits, an archival center, and a Hall of Fame.

The other major strand of the project was educational, and here Fender wanted to offer free and low-cost performing-arts teaching. The Kids Rock Free program provided lessons for 400 children per week for various instruments and for singing – at first with a year-and-a-half waiting list – but this, too, was designed to expand.

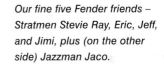

● *Main guitar: This Jaco Pastorius Jazz Bass, in Sunburst, was made in 1999. An aged Tribute version, replicating Jaco's own road-weary Jazz, was available from the Custom Shop.*

Our fine five Fender friends – Stratmen Stevie Ray, Eric, Jeff, and Jimi, plus (on the other side) Jazzman Jaco.

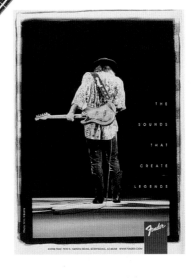

"Into the 21st century, Fender was the most powerful name in guitar-land, still making great instruments that musicians wanted as much as ever."

00s

2000
Fifty and counting

Decades on from its earliest solidbody instruments, Fender honored its founder with the Leo Fender Broadcaster (main guitar), celebrating the 50th anniversary of the elegantly simple and remarkably resilient Tele design. Tele and Strat continued to enthuse new bands – like Coldplay (above) – while classic successes were trumpeted in ads like this one (right). Elsewhere, there were new models, too, as Fender pushed ahead with baritones, seven-strings, and fiberglass bodies.

As the old millennium passed and the 21st century dawned, Fender like the rest of the world took the opportunity to look back. Full of respect for its glorious past, Fender was nonetheless curious about the mysteries that might lie ahead in the years and decades to come.

From the past came a link to one of the greatest bluesmen ever. Muddy Waters, who'd died back in 1983 at the age of 70, is forever associated with the Telecaster he used almost from the moment he went electric and started to tear up the music. Fender's Tribute Series provided the framework for a nitpicking replica of that famous instrument, collected today among the other exhibits at Cleveland's Rock & Roll Hall Of Fame.

George Blanda from Fender's Custom Shop took precise measurements of Muddy's original candy apple red 1960s Telecaster, with its retrofitted custom neck and Fender amp knobs. There's no denying its relevance to the Tribute Series, which Fender described as its "elite program," specifying: "Each instrument selected played an integral part in the development of the artist, and helped shape and influence the historical significance of his or her music." Only 100 instruments were produced, beginning in April this year, and each came with a tweed case, a limited-edition poster, a CD of Muddy's music, and other signature accessories. Further new models this year included a few shortlived models:

the seven-string Showmaster, and various 27-inch-scale Sub-Sonic baritone Strat and Tele variations. The Double Fat Strat boasted two Seymour Duncan humbuckers – a pickup combination that in earlier decades would have been seen as the antithesis of Stratocaster – while the Telecoustic and Stratacoustic were new thinline electro-acoustics with spruce tops and fiberglass backs and sides. This marked a typical move for Fender, using an exciting new material but in the context of its safe, most famous body shapes. Meanwhile, the Classic Rocker was a distinctly Gretsch-like semi foreshadowing the official link between Fender and Gretsch that would take place in the next few years.

Also this year, there was a change of name for Fender's bestselling American Standard guitars, which had first launched back in 1986. The various models became simply 'American', dropping the Standard. Fender officially unveiled the new series of Precision and Jazz Bass, Strat, and Tele at the historic RCA recording studio in Nashville in July. It described the new models as "evolutionary," but there seemed little that was different apart from the name in the catalog. The slight shift of name would last until 2008, when all was changed back to American Standard once again.

● *Main guitar: This Leo Fender Broadcaster, #44 of 50, marked the original model's 50th anniversary. A certificate and documents (below left) came with it.*

The mix of old and new continues: Thom Yorke of Radiohead is pictured (above) with a 70s-style Tele Deluxe.

A limited-run aged Custom Shop guitar (below) was made this year in tribute to Muddy Waters and his Telecaster.

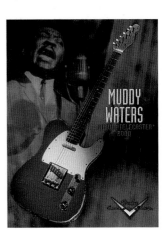

The Classic Rocker (right) was a notably Gretsch-like hollowbody, new this year.

P-Bass B-day

Fender celebrated the simplicity of the Precision Bass, 50 years old this year, with replicas from the Custom Shop and the US factory, while Tom Delonge of blink-182 made a mark with modern simplicity. His signature model was a stripped-down Strat with one pickup and one control. Meanwhile, Ryan Adams (playing a Tele Deluxe, above) hit with his song 'New York, New York' in the aftermath of the terrorist attacks on the US.

This year marked the 50th anniversary of the most revolutionary instrument that Fender ever introduced, the Precision Bass, and the company made sure that news of the birthday did not escape attention, releasing two anniversary models.

The first was made in the Custom Shop, which built the limited-edition 1951 Anniversary Precision Bass to exacting specs. The Shop did its usual careful job, copying the original as closely as possible, right down to small details such as "step-drilled" tuner holes, a fiber pickguard and fingerboard dots, phenolic bridge saddles, and even a form-fit chipboard case. The factory-production 50th Anniversary American Series Precision was a more generic P-Bass, not based on the original '51 style. Neither model should be confused with the later-style Precision 50th anniversary model made in a numbered edition of 500 in 1996, complete with its gold anniversary sticker on the headstock marking the company's birthday.

Modeling was a new technology applied to guitar-playing as musicians entered the 21st century. The idea is to provide digital re-creations of classic guitar and amp sounds. California-based Line 6 was the leader, and its Vetta amps and Pod boxes showed what could be done. Other amp makers followed and, naturally, leaned heavily on the sounds of classic Fender models.

It was inevitable that Fender itself would enter this brave new world, which it did with its own take on the idea of multiple amp sounds, the Cyber Twin 2x12 130-watt combo (upgraded in 2004 as the Cyber Twin SE). Fender later issued a number of derivatives using the same "Cybernetic Amp Design" technology, and launched a budget practice-amp line in 2005, the G-DEC series, that also featured amp simulations.

Simplicity and accessibility seemed the admirable rationale behind the Tom Delonge Stratocaster, launched to match the guitar that Delonge used regularly with his band blink-182. The Mexican-made production model duplicated the guitarist's straightforward requirement of a single Seymour Duncan humbucker, a large 1970s-style headstock, and just the one control knob: for volume, of course. Delonge explained he didn't need more pickups and knobs – but that he wanted to simply plug in and play!

Up at the legendary end of Fender's signature series, two models had a change of pickups this year, which, said Fender, reflected alterations made by the artists themselves to their own guitars. The Eric Clapton Strat gained Vintage Noiseless pickups, while the Jeff Beck Strat was fitted with Ceramic Noiseless units, in both cases replacing the existing Lace Sensors.

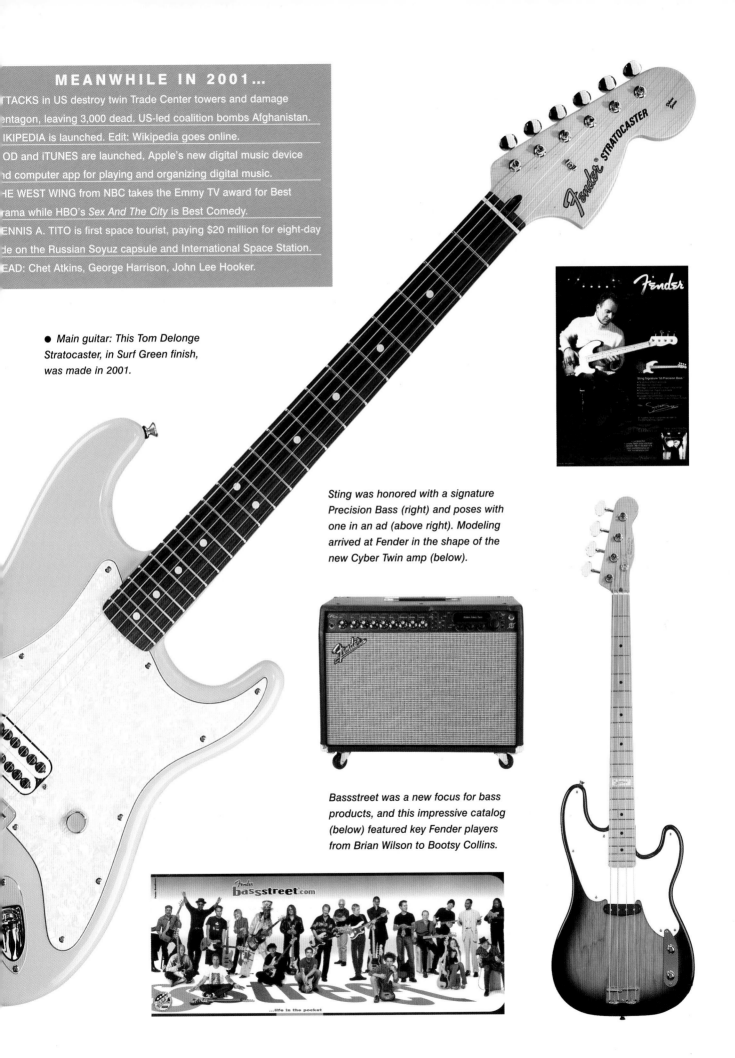

● *Main guitar: This Tom Delonge
Stratocaster, in Surf Green finish,
was made in 2001.*

*Sting was honored with a signature
Precision Bass (right) and poses with
one in an ad (above right). Modeling
arrived at Fender in the shape of the
new Cyber Twin amp (below).*

*Bassstreet was a new focus for bass
products, and this impressive catalog
(below) featured key Fender players
from Brian Wilson to Bootsy Collins.*

Guild-alikes

Fender had not been slow in acquiring other brands, and this year the company added Jackson/Charvel to the portfolio as well as launching a shortlived set of Squier Guild-alike electric models. New to the US-made models were the Highway One Strat and Tele, with thin "satin" vintage-looking finishes and a classic vibe. Craig Nicholls with Australia's post-grungers The Vines divided his time between playing his Strat (above) and smashing it into the drum kit.

The Squier brand was 20 years old this year, and Fender marked the anniversary by fitting a commemorative neckplate to many models. The neckplate read: "20th Anniversary Squier By Fender: Freedom Of Expression Since 1982." Fender also launched a new Squier line of guitars, called Series 24 and named for its 24¾-inch scale length – usually associated with Gibson guitars rather than Fender, which customarily use a 25½-inch scale.

A more accurate name would have been the Squier Guild electrics. Fender had acquired Guild back in 1995, and the idea with Series 24 was to create a budget-price line of Guild-style electrics that would complement Squier's existing Fender derivatives. Thus the solidbody M-50, M-70, and M-77 mirrored Guild's old M-series and the S-65 and S-73 the old S-series, while the X-155 and Starfire were semi-acoustic electrics again based on classic Guild models. It seemed that players didn't want this kind of thing from Squier, however, and most were gone in a few years, although the X-155 lasted to 2005.

Fender continued to acquire famous brandnames, this year buying Jackson/Charvel from its present owner, Akai. Fender's deal gave it the inventory, trademarks, and designs along with the Jackson/Charvel factory in California that made custom and limited-edition instruments. It must have been satisfying for Fender management now to own the brands that had done so much to rival

Fender when Jackson and Charvel spearheaded the superstrat trends of the 1980s.

Absorbed with its peripheral models, Fender took a further look at several of its 'new' guitar shapes this year, launching a handful of variations on the Cyclone and Toronado models, both originally introduced four years ago. The new Cyclone II kept the original's body shape and trem, but added Competition Mustang body stripes, changed the pickups to three Jaguar single-coils, and provided a three-switch Jag-like control panel. Two new American Special takes on the offset-waist Toronado shape offered Gibson-like features, including two soapbars or open humbuckers, a smaller pickguard, and a separate bridge and bar tailpiece. None of these changes did much to improve the popularity of the Cyclone or the Toronado, and by 2006 all the variations had been deleted from the various catalogs and pricelists.

Maybe the work on the Cyclone II reminded Fender of its old Mustang models. Japanese-made Mustang Bass reissues appeared this year, as well as a shortlived Competition Mustang six-string reissue offered with the distinctive striped-body finishes first seen back in 1968.

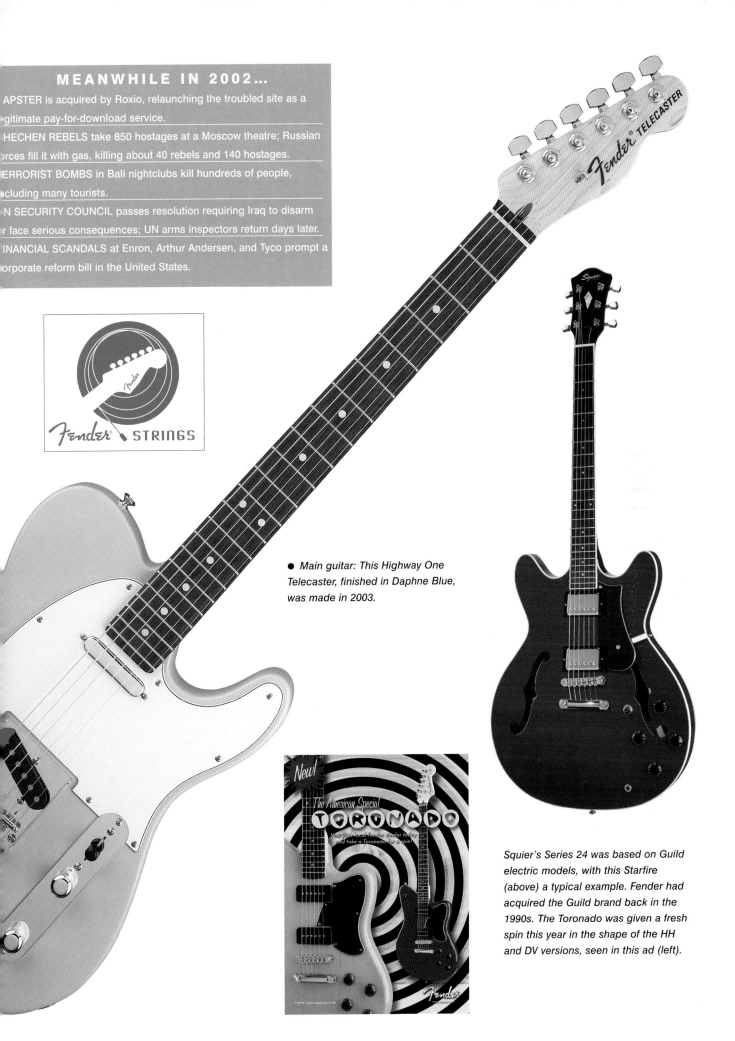

● *Main guitar: This Highway One Telecaster, finished in Daphne Blue, was made in 2003.*

Squier's Series 24 was based on Guild electric models, with this Starfire (above) a typical example. Fender had acquired the Guild brand back in the 1990s. The Toronado was given a fresh spin this year in the shape of the HH and DV versions, seen in this ad (left).

2003
Shall we switch?

Still acquisitive, Fender started to work an alliance with Gretsch that meant that Fender finally had some decent semis. It was another signature-crazy year, adding Mark Knopfler, Marcus Miller, Robert Cray (above), and Jimmy Bryant. Meanwhile, John Mayer, who released his Heavier Things album (right), had to wait a couple of years for his signature Strat.

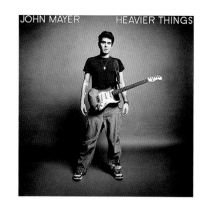

A new pickup-switching system arrived on several new models, including the HSS and HH Strats and the HH and HS Teles, and it was gradually added to some existing American and Deluxe guitars and basses. The S-1 is a simple option on the master volume knob, but the results are as complex as you want. The new HSS Strat, for example, had a bridge humbucker plus two single-coils, and the guitar's five-way selector worked more or less as you'd expect with the S-1 switch in the up position. With it down, several new combinations were available, including all three pickups on, with both or just one of the humbucker coils engaged. The S-1 provided tonal heaven or pickup mayhem, depending on your taste.

In a big year for new models, signature instruments continued to appear – everything from a Mark Knopfler Strat to a Marcus Miller five-string Jazz Bass – but it was the Telecaster that perhaps offered the most surprising extremes. At one end was the Jimmy Bryant model (above). You'll recall that Bryant, a brilliant West Coast session man, was one of the first to test-drive and popularize the original Broadcaster back in 1950. Bryant, who died in 1980, was honored this year by Fender with a Custom Shop Telecaster, which had a hand-tooled leather pickguard in Bryant's favoured elaborate style.

At the other end of the scale were the two J5 Telecasters, made for Marilyn Manson guitarist John 5 (John Lowery) and described by Fender as "equal parts shocking, rocking, and versatile." The differences to a regular Tele came in the form of a shaved neck, the pickups, and a very un-Fender three-tuners-each-side headstock. The new models were the J5:HB, with bridge humbucker and neck single-coil, and the J5: Bigsby, with two single-coils and vibrato. Later, a Mexico-made version of the HB appeared and a three-humbucker Triple Tele Deluxe with Strat-style headstock. John 5 would leave Manson in 2005 to work with Rob Zombie.

John Page, who helped establish the Custom Shop, had moved to set up the Fender Museum of Music & The Arts Foundation, but he left Fender in January this year, relocating to Oregon to build furniture and guitars.

Fender made an alliance with Gretsch at the end of last year and put it into operation. With Guild and now Gretsch under its umbrella, Fender at last found a way to overcome its historically uncertain attempts to make decent and accepted flat-top acoustics and archtop electric-acoustics. Gretsch appeared to prosper in the new environment, and many improved models began to appear over the coming years.

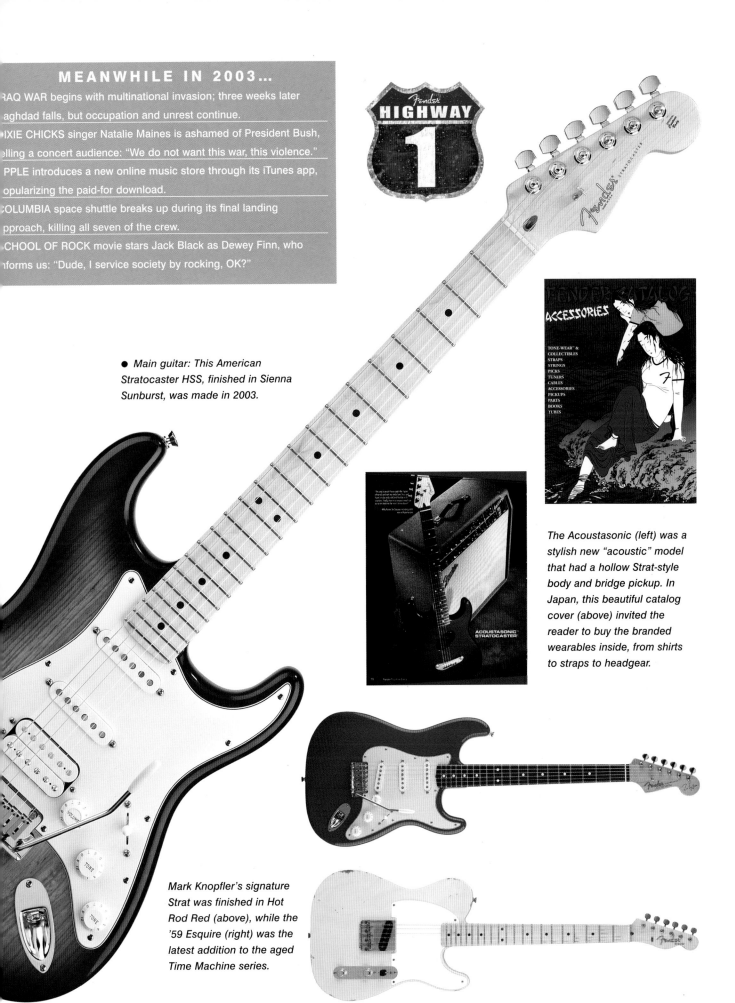

● *Main guitar: This American Stratocaster HSS, finished in Sienna Sunburst, was made in 2003.*

The Acoustasonic (left) was a stylish new "acoustic" model that had a hollow Strat-style body and bridge pickup. In Japan, this beautiful catalog cover (above) invited the reader to buy the branded wearables inside, from shirts to straps to headgear.

Mark Knopfler's signature Strat was finished in Hot Rod Red (above), while the '59 Esquire (right) was the latest addition to the aged Time Machine series.

2004
Happy Stratday

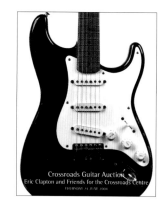

The Stratocaster turned a vivacious, thriving 50, and Fender celebrated with a birthday concert in London where David Gilmour (above) completed the six-string circle by playing his revered early Strat with serial-number 0001. Eric Clapton was another guitarist who had fun with history this year, selling his equally revered Blackie Strat for just short of a million dollars at auction (catalogue, right), with the proceeds benefiting his drug rehab charity.

Crossroads Guitar Auction
Eric Clapton and Friends for the Crossroads Centre
THURSDAY 24 JUNE 2004

The main signs of this year's 50th birthday of the Stratocaster came with four special anniversary models and a celebratory concert at London's Wembley Arena. The show featured David Gilmour and Hank Marvin, unquestionably Strat men, along with a good number of other guitarists less well-known for their Strat associations. Some of the audience might have expected to see Eric Clapton or Jeff Beck but instead were offered Amy Winehouse, Paul Rodgers, Theresa Andersson, and the rest.

Clapton may not have been at the Wembley bash, but he sold his most famous Stratocaster, Blackie, for a record-breaking sum at auction. Clapton acquired Blackie toward the end of 1970, adapting parts from three 1950s Strats to make what became his most cherished instrument until the mid 1980s. Guitar Center, the US music-store chain, bought it at Christie's in New York City in June for a record-breaking $959,000 (plus buyer's premium), benefiting Clapton's Crossroads charity.

Fender's four 50th anniversary Strats were crowned by a no-detail-spared Custom Shop replica 1954 Stratocaster, listed as a Limited Release at an appropriate $5,400. "Every deep body contour, pickup magnet, and screw is a replica of a 1954 Strat," said Fender. "We even went as far as having pre-CBS Fender employee Roger Centeno stamp each tremolo cover plate with the original die."

Fender's original publicity back in 1954 said: "For tone, appearance, and versatility, the Stratocaster has been engineered to give the player every possible advantage." As you will notice as you read this book, that's been so throughout much of the ensuing 50 years and still seems to be in place today.

Down a notch came two more birthday Strats, the American Series and the American Deluxe 50th Anniversary models, both with identifying neckplates, assorted modern features, and the Deluxe with suitable gold-plated hardware. Last, there was the Mexico-made 50th Anniversary Golden Stratocaster, which lived up to its name, with Aztec Gold finish, gold-plated hardware, and gold-anodized pickguard.

In the workaday Fender department, the American Deluxe models were upgraded this year with new SCN (Somarium Cobalt Noiseless) pickups by veteran designer Bill Lawrence, and S-1 pickup-switching system. Traditional materials graced the Deluxe Ash Strat and Tele, while more Showmaster models appeared, including the Elite Standard in HH or HSS formats, and a Bass Amplification department was established. Squier added to its Vintage Modified series with the unusual but engaging '51 model, essentially a Telecaster but with 1951 P-Bass-style pickguard and control plate, plus a humbucker at the bridge and slanted single-coil at the neck.

● *Main guitar: This
Showmaster Elite FMT, in
Cherry Sunburst finish,
was made in 2004.*

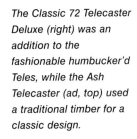

*The Classic 72 Telecaster
Deluxe (right) was an
addition to the
fashionable humbucker'd
Teles, while the Ash
Telecaster (ad, top) used
a traditional timber for a
classic design.*

*The 50th Anniversary Golden
(right) was a Mexico-made
Strat with an appropriately
golden sheen. Mike Dirnt of
Green Day (far right) had a
signature P-Bass out this year.*

2005
Count those frets

A few more anniversaries this year: it was ten years since the Time Machine guitars appeared and proved that old could really be new; and it was twenty years since Fender management bought the company from CBS and began reorganizing itself into a modern operation. Those past achievements fueled some good new models this year, including the Korean-made Jazz 24 (right), which was Fender's first 24-fret Jazz Bass. Chris Walla of Death Cab For Cutie (above) meanwhile chose an old Starcaster.

Ten years on from its introduction, and the Time Machine series – Fender's aged and vintage-like new guitars – had blossomed into an important part of the Custom Shop's business.

Since 1998, the series was offered in three levels of ageing. N.O.S. (New Old Stock) models are intended as pristine replicas of original brand-new instruments from a particular year. Closet Classics are like guitars bought new years ago, played a little, then shoved in a closet. Relics have the full aged look, with dings and wear added by the Shop to resemble a well-played oldie.

This year saw the Time Machines settle down to a line that featured nine models: a '51 Nocaster, a '63 and '67 Telecaster, a '59 Esquire, and Stratocasters for '56, '60, '65, '66, and '69; plus a '64 Jazz Bass and Precisions for '55 and '59.

The busy folk in the Custom Shop also continued to produce their upscale one-off 'art' guitars, including this year such delights as the Fender Memorabilia Set, created by artist Dave Newman on a Stratocaster made by Master Builder Chris Fleming, which Newman covered in a fascinating collage of vintage Fender catalogues and ads. The set was completed by a similarly decorated Blues Junior amp.

"We've worked with several artists to really make the 'art guitar' moniker more true," said Mike Eldred, the Shop's director of sales and marketing. "Shepard Fairey, Pamelina, Shag, and Crash are just some of the artists we continue to work with, offering them a new and unique palette."

The highest and lowest levels of Fender's operation – the lofty Custom Shop and the budget Squier brand – met in the new Squier Master Series. The Squier M-80, designed by the Custom Shop, was a development of the Series 24 guitars, with set-neck and twin humbuckers, while the Esprit was based on the original 1984 design.

Fender Japan was reorganized early in 2005 when a new company, Dyna Boeki, was formed to produce Fender's Japanese instruments. Fender said that this was a tidying-up of the business arrangements and that nothing about the physical production of the guitars changed.

At the same time they simplified distribution: now all Japanese-made instruments were distributed in Japan by Kanda Shokai, while the rest of the Fender and Squier catalogue made in the US and elsewhere was distributed by Yamano Music.

New Japan-made guitars this year included a pair of interesting Jaguar-derived models, the two-humbucker HH and a low-tuned, long-scale Baritone version of the same instrument.

● *Main guitar: This '67 Telecaster N.O.S., finished in Black, was made in 2005. It was part of the Time Machine series: N.O.S. means New Old Stock, designed to look like a "brand new" vintage oldie.*

Mary Kaye (far left) plays the Tribute version of her famous blond/gold Strat. A Custom Shop art set (above) had a Fender memorabilia finish.

The unusual Squier M-80 (left) and a catalog entry for the Standard Stratocaster FMT model (above).

2006
Godlike tribute

There was a 60th birthday to celebrate this year, and plenty of famous Fender users lined up to pass on their good wishes to the company, including Avril Lavigne (above left) with her fine checkered Tele. Meanwhile, Eric Clapton's Blackie got the Tribute treatment, and a new line of acoustics appeared, the mid-price California Series (ad, above).

This year marked the 60th anniversary of Leo's original Fender Manufacturing company. The modern Fender Musical Instruments Corporation, known as FMIC, took the opportunity to blow its own trumpet – or, more likely, to strum its own guitar. "Fender is now the single largest and most successful manufacturer of electric guitars, basses, and amplifiers in the world," it claimed in a press release. "In addition to the Fender brandname, FMIC markets under the brandnames Squier, Guild, Jackson, Charvel, SWR, Tacoma, Olympia, Orpheum, Gretsch, and Rodriguez. The company operates directly in more than 12 countries around the globe … and it maintains its own state-of-the-art manufacturing facilities in California, Washington, and Ensenada, Mexico."

Upstairs in the boardroom, Bill Schultz had stepped down as Fender CEO in 2005, staying on as chairman of the board of directors, and Bill Mendello became CEO. Sadly, Schultz died in September 2006. Dan Smith waved goodbye to Fender this year after 25 remarkable years with the company, including the crucial management buy-out from CBS in 1985 and the creative struggle through the years immediately following. "Part of being able to retire," Smith said, "was that I knew we'd accomplished a lot. And the heart of the company is always the product. I could walk away proud, knowing Fender was so far ahead of where it had

been, in terms of technology and training and people, and that it was going to continue and go way beyond that."

A special entry in the Tribute Series came with the Eric Clapton Blackie Stratocaster. Blackie was the guitar that Clapton acquired in 1970, made from three old Strats to become his most cherished axe until the 1980s. Guitar Center, the music-store chain, bought Blackie from Clapton at auction in 2004 for a record-breaking $959,000 (plus buyer's premium), benefiting Clapton's Crossroads drug-rehab charity.

The new owner allowed the Custom Shop access to the instrument in 2005 so that Fender could spec the historic Strat for the exacting Tribute replicas. Just 275 were made, of which 185 were sold through Guitar Center and the rest through Fender's international channels. Guitar Center sold all theirs in one day, with 106 going in the first two minutes. The suggested retail price was $24,000 each, with a portion donated to the Crossroads Centre in Antigua and a new facility in Delray Beach, Florida.

More affordable was the new line of Squier Hello Kitty instruments, which featured the Japanese cultural icon and with which, according to Fender, "We hope to show young women just how much fun playing the guitar can be." Now don't get serious, girls.

● *Main guitar: This Eric Clapton Blackie Stratocaster was one of the 2006 limited edition of 275.*

Arctic Monkeys (above) released their debut album to great acclaim this year, with firm Fender fans Alex Turner (Strat, left) and James Cook (Tele) in charge of six-strings.

This Squier Affinity (above) was one of a line of Hello Kitty guitars, while the Highway One HSS Strat (below) was another Fender with the versatile humbucker-plus-two-single-coils layout.

Strat modeling

The modeling guitar came to Fender's line in the shape of a new American VG Stratocaster (below), featured on the cover of the regular Frontline catalogue (right), while Vintage Hot Rod models combined classic styling with modern playability. Radiohead, who continued with their Fender-flavored guitar sound, raised eyebrows by offering a "pay what you like" album download. Jonny Greenwood is pictured (above) manhandling a paid-for Tele.

Fender staged its first Hall Of Fame event, suitably on the day that Leo Fender would have been 98. Leo himself was honored, of course, alongside Don Randall, Bill Schultz, Freddie Tavares, Forrest White, and Charlie Hayes – names you'll know from earlier in this book. Leo's second wife, Phyllis Fender, accepted the award, saying: "Every day in this world, completely around this world, when a musician picks up one of Leo's dreams and holds that guitar in his arms and strums it, and plays a few chords ... Leo is alive, and Leo's dream goes on and on."

Today, one of the recurring aims at Fender is to make what everyone seems to want: a vintage-style instrument with features to suit the modern player. Last year, the Classic Player series built on the idea, combining Custom Shop know-how with Mexican production, and the budget Squier brand's Vintage Modified series had similar intentions. Now it was the turn of the higher-end and the new US-made Vintage Hot Rod guitars. They were based on US-made vintage reissues but offered thin-skin lacquer finishes, flatter fingerboards, bigger frets, modern pickups, and custom wiring. The series kicked off with a '57 and '62 Strat and '52 Tele.

"Everyone likes the look and feel of a vintage Fender," said marketing manager Justin Norvell, "but many want it to play like a modern instrument. Plus, many vintage guitar owners are hesitant to reduce the value by making the desired modifications, so here is a guitar that solves that problem outright."

California-based Line 6 had already showed what could be done with digital modeling, recreating classic guitar and amp sounds, and Fender's Cyber-Twin amp had been around for a few years. The company's take on the modeling guitar was the American VG Stratocaster, created in collaboration with Japanese hi-tech company Roland. Unlike some competitors, Fender did everything inside the instrument: the only connection needed was a regular jack to a regular amp.

Two extra knobs on the VG Strat controlled the new sounds, together with a small LED and a Roland GK bridge pickup. The Mode Control knob provided five sound settings for a variety of real and modeled guitar tones, and the Tuning Control knob offered a range of instant alternative tunings. The VG lasted only to 2009.

In other news, there was a Joe Strummer Tribute Tele, honoring the Clash guitar man, an announcement of the EVH brand, teaming the Custom Shop's master builders with guitar wizard Eddie Van Halen, and Fender acquired Kaman, the firm responsible for Ovation and Hamer guitars.

● *Main guitar: This J. Mascis
Jazzmaster, finished in Purple
Sparkle, was made in 2007.*

*Two striking logos: one for the new
VG modeling Strat (top), the other
(right) marking this year's 20th
birthday of the Custom Shop.*

*A catalog shot (above) of a '51 Nocaster
Closet Classic and a Champion 600 amp
recalled Fender's earliest days. The Tribute
series remembered Joe Strummer with this
copy of The Clash man's ragged Tele (right).*

● *Main guitar: This left-hand American Standard Stratocaster, finished in Candy Cola, was made in 2008.*

Fender added more models to its Vintage Reissue amps, including this sparkling '65 Princeton Reverb (below).

It was the 50th anniversary of the Jazzmaster model, and Fender staged a special concert (poster, above) to celebrate. An unusual interpretation of the classic design came with the Jazzmaster-Coustic (below).

2008
Mastering jazz

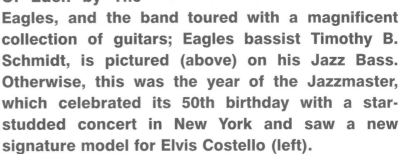

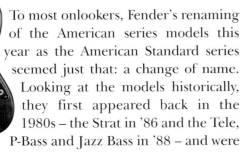

One of the year's bestselling albums was Long Road Out Of Eden by The Eagles, and the band toured with a magnificent collection of guitars; Eagles bassist Timothy B. Schmidt, is pictured (above) on his Jazz Bass. Otherwise, this was the year of the Jazzmaster, which celebrated its 50th birthday with a star-studded concert in New York and saw a new signature model for Elvis Costello (left).

To most onlookers, Fender's renaming of the American series models this year as the American Standard series seemed just that: a change of name. Looking at the models historically, they first appeared back in the 1980s – the Strat in '86 and the Tele, P-Bass and Jazz Bass in '88 – and were intended to provide the new US-made core of the Fender line. They started life then as American Standards, but trimmed the name to pure and simple American in 2000. Now, Fender talked of new finishes, improved bridges, tinted necks, and parchment pickguards and knobs that, combined, provided the refreshed American Standards with a "more expensive" look.

Some of the best Fender amps of recent years have appeared in the carefully revived line of reissue models, and this year saw the appearance of the '65 Princeton Reverb. The original had been intended as a small practice amp, but nonetheless the little unit packed some big tone, and Fender claimed the reissue offered an affordable and roadworthy alternative to originals, which had become further entries in the valuable Fender collectables market.

Fender announced a new education program, the so-called Fender University. Places were limited –

a mere 35 to begin with – and the intention seemed to be to combine workshops and performances with hands-on access to Fender's factory and Custom Shop.

Don Randall died at the age of 91. If you've ever played a Fender guitar, you owe a lot to him. You know from this book that Don together with Leo made the original Fender company happen, and Don also came up with nearly all the classic model names, including Telecaster and Stratocaster.

The Jazzmaster turned 50 this year, and Fender organized another celebratory concert like the one held for the Strat a few years back. It was staged at New York City's Knitting Factory club and featured well-known Jazzmaster players including Thurston Moore of Sonic Youth, J Mascis of Dinosaur Jr, Nels Cline of Wilco, and Tom Verlaine of Television. More unusual was the new Jazzmaster-Coustic model (facing page, bottom).

A few Jazzmaster signature models appeared around the anniversary, including a guitar this year for Elvis Costello, replicating his Jazzmaster (above left) as it existed upon his rise to fame in the late 1970s. "This is a brutal-sounding guitar," said Costello. "It suits the way I play. But this guitar … it's had a funny life. And I've just always stuck with it; I always come back to it. I've done all sorts of different music, but whenever it's involved electric guitar, I don't think there's one record I've made on which the Jazzmaster doesn't feature somewhere."

Sixty years on from the first Fender solidbody guitars, those early designs continue to inspire artists-of-the-moment – such as Biffy Clyro's Simon Neil (left). Fender tries today to provide models that will appeal to every conceivable type of guitarist and bassist at all levels of skill and affluence. Despite the constant references to past achievements (ad, right), the future might well have in store a new and unimagined direction for Fender and for music.

Today, the Fender Musical Instruments Corporation dominates the world's electric guitar market. As we've seen, it arrived here through a sequence of invention, luck and mishap. Back in the 1950s when the whole adventure started, a Strat was a Strat, and that's what you bought. Now, popular music has fractured into dozens of different factions, each apparently requiring a specific instrument. In 2009, there were 41 distinct factory-made Stratocaster models available.

Sixty years is a long time for a company to survive in any business. Fender has seen its share of shaky times – not least in the earliest days when the company regularly avoided a calamity by the timely arrival of Leo's wife's salary from the phone company. No doubt Leo would be in awe if he could see the modern Fender operation (though he'd still feel that this pickup or that amp could be improved). It was his determination – today it would probably be described as workaholicism – that guided much of the company's early direction. Of course, he listened to what musicians had to say to him. And he assembled a first-rate team: the Don Randalls and Freddie Tavares's and Forrest Whites of those crucial, ground-breaking days in Fullerton.

No other guitar-making company has scored with such an impressive trio of early products. The Telecaster, as it quickly became known, is a historic instrument: the world's first modern commercially-available solidbody electric Spanish guitar. The Stratocaster is the most influential solidbody design ever, beating even Gibson's mighty Les Paul into second place. And Fender's most revolutionary product was the Precision Bass, the first commercial electric bass guitar and an instrument that changed the sound of popular music.

And all that within four years. More models followed in the wake of that great trio, of course: a few were very good, some were clearly bad, others simply indifferent. But Fender's sheer exhilarating invention between 1950 and 1954 is still astounding. All musicians, all guitar-makers, all music fans are in debt to what Leo Fender and his team achieved in those years.

Back in 1950 – a year of innocence and excitement at Fender as that first solidbody guitar appeared – someone, probably Don Randall, wrote a short note in the catalog: "The Fender people hope to always be close to the feelings of those who buy, sell and play electric instruments, because that is the greatest source of information for the development and improvement of instruments." Nothing much has changed since, and yet everything has changed.

● *Main guitar: This Road
Worn 60s Jazz Bass,
finished in Fiesta Red, was
made in 2009. The new
Mexico-made series
brought the Time Machine
"aged" idea to more
affordable instruments.*

*These covers (below) of the 2009
pricelists for basses (left) and electric
guitars (right) have Fender stressing,
once again, that the history of the brand
is forever renewing itself.*

*There were yet more signature
models to add to the list this
year. The Mexico-made Ritchie
Blackmore Stratocaster (above)
had the master's distinctive
scalloped fingerboard, while
Sonic Youth's two guitarists
Thurston Moore and Lee
Ranaldo (left) posed with their
new signature Jazzmasters.*

chronology 1950-2009

This list shows in chronological order the production-model electric guitars and basses with "Fender" as the main logo or brandname, manufactured in the US, Japan, Korea and Mexico, from 1950 to 2009.

The start date shown is the year that production commenced for each model in the country of manufacture, and the finish date is the final year that each model was available in the US, Europe or both.

Broadcaster	1950–51
Esquire	1950–69
Nocaster	1951
Precision Bass (1st version)	1951–57
Telecaster	1951–83
Stratocaster (pre-CBS)	1954–65
Duo-Sonic (1st version)	1956–64
Musicmaster (1st version)	1956–64
Precision Bass (2nd version)	1957–81
Jazzmaster	1958–80
Custom Esquire	1959–69
Custom Telecaster	1959–72
Jazz Bass (1st version)	1960–62
VI (aka "Bass VI") (1st version)	1961–63
Jaguar	1962–75
Jazz Bass (2nd version)	1962–75
VI (aka "Bass VI") (2nd version)	1963–75
Duo-Sonic (2nd version)	1964–69
Duo-Sonic II	1964–69
Musicmaster (2nd version)	1964–75
Musicmaster II	1964–69
Mustang (regular scale)	1964–81
Mustang (short scale)	1964–69
Bass V	1965–70
Electric XII	1965–69
Stratocaster (CBS Sixties)	1965–71
Coronado I	1966–69
Coronado I Bass	1966–68
Coronado II	1966–69
Coronado XII	1966–69

Mustang Bass	1966–81
Slab-Body Precision Bass	1966–67
Bronco	1967–80
Coronado II Antigua	1967–71
Coronado II Bass	1967–69
Coronado II Wildwood	1967–69
Coronado II Wildwood Bass	1967–69
Coronado XII Antigua	1967–71
Coronado XII Wildwood	1967–69
Blue Flower Telecaster	1968–69
Blue Flower Telecaster Bass	1968–69
Competition Mustang	1968–73
Competition Mustang Bass	1968–73
Coronado II Antigua Bass	1968–71
LTD	1968–74
Montego I	1968–74
Montego II	1968–74
Paisley Red Telecaster	1968–69
Paisley Red Telecaster Bass	1968–69
Telecaster Bass (1st version)	1968–72
Thinline Telecaster (1st version)	1968–71
Custom (aka Maverick)	1969–70
Musicmaster (2nd version)	1969–75
Rosewood Telecaster	1969–72
Swinger (aka Arrow or Musiclander)	1969
Musicmaster Bass	1970–81
Stratocaster (CBS Seventies)	1971–81
Thinline Telecaster (2nd version)	1971–79
Telecaster Bass (2nd version)	1972–78
Telecaster Custom	1972–81
Telecaster Deluxe	1973–81
Jazz Bass (3rd version)	1975–81
Musicmaster (3rd version)	1975–80
Rhinestone Stratocaster	1975

Starcaster	1976–80
Antigua Jazz Bass	1977–79
Antigua Mustang	1977–79
Antigua Mustang Bass	1977–79
Antigua Precision Bass	1977–79
Antigua Stratocaster	1977–79
Antigua Telecaster	1977–79
Antigua Telecaster Custom	1977–79
Antigua Telecaster Deluxe	1977–79
Lead I	1979–82
Lead II	1979–82
25th Anniversary Stratocaster	1979–80
Hendrix Stratocaster	1980
Precision Special Bass	1980–83
Strat	1980–83
Walnut Precision Special Bass	1980–83
Black & Gold Telecaster	1981–83
Bullet (1st version)	1981–83
Bullet Deluxe	1981–83
Gold/Gold Jazz Bass	1981–83
Gold/Gold Stratocaster	1981–83
International Color Jazz Bass	1981
International Color Precision Bass	1981
International Color Stratocaster	1981
International Color Telecaster	1981
Jazz Bass Standard (1st version)	1981–83
Lead III	1981–82
Precision Bass Standard (1st version)	1981–83
Stratocaster Standard (1st version)	1981–83
Walnut Strat	1981–83
Bullet B-30 Bass	1982–83
Bullet B-34 Bass	1982–83
Squier Series '62 Jazz Bass (J)	1982–83
Squier Series '57 Precision Bass (J)	1982–83
Squier Series '62 Precision Bass (J)	1982–83
Squier Series '57 Stratocaster (J)	1982–83
Squier Series '62 Stratocaster (J)	1982–83
Squier Series '52 Telecaster (J)	1982–83

Model	Years
'62 Jazz Bass	1982–98
'57 Precision Bass	1982–98
'62 Precision Bass	1982–98
60s Jazz Bass (J)	1982–94
50s Precision Bass (J)	1982–94
60s Precision Bass (J)	1982–94
Bullet (2nd version)	1983
Bullet H1	1983
Bullet H2	1983
Bullet S2	1983
Bullet S3	1983
Elite Precision Bass	1983–85
Elite II Precision Bass	1983–85
Elite Stratocaster	1983–84
Elite Telecaster	1983–84
Gold Elite Precision Bass	1983–85
Gold Elite II Precision Bass	1983–85
Gold Elite Stratocaster	1983–84
Gold Elite Telecaster	1983–84
Jazz Bass Standard (2nd version)	1983–85
Precision Bass Standard (2nd version)	1983–85
Stratocaster Standard (2nd version)	1983–84
Telecaster Standard	1983–84
Walnut Elite II Precision Bass	1983–85
Walnut Elite Stratocaster	1983–84
Walnut Elite Telecaster	1983–84
'52 Telecaster	1983–84, 86–98
'57 Stratocaster	1983–85, 86–98
'62 Stratocaster	1983–85, 86–98
Bowling Ball Stratocaster (aka Marble Stratocaster)	1984
Bowling Ball Telecaster (aka Marble Telecaster)	1984
D'Aquisto Elite (J)	1984, 1989–94
D'Aquisto Standard (J)	1984
Esprit (Standard, Elite, Ultra) (J)	1984
Flame (Standard, Elite, Ultra) (J)	1984
Contemporary Jazz Bass Special (aka P-J, Jazz Special) (J)	1985–91
Contemporary Precision Bass (J)	1985–87
Contemporary Stratocaster (4 variations) (J)	1985–87
Contemporary Stratocaster Deluxe (2 variations) (J)	1985–87
Contemporary Telecaster (2 variations) (J)	1985–87
Custom Telecaster '62 (J)	1985–onward
Katana (J)	1985–86
Performer (J)	1985–86
Performer Bass (J)	1985–86
Standard Stratocaster (1st version) (J)	1985–89
Stratocaster '72 (J)	1985–onward
50s Stratocaster (J)	1985–onward
60s Stratocaster (J)	1985–onward
American Standard Stratocaster (1st version)	1986–2000
Blue Flower Telecaster (J)	1986–onward
Custom Esquire (J)	1986–onward
Esquire (J)	1986–onward
Jaguar (J)	1986–onward
Jazzmaster (J)	1986–onward
Mustang (J)	1986–onward
Paisley Telecaster (J)	1986–onward
Rosewood Telecaster (J)	1986–onward
Telecaster Custom '72 (J)	1986–onward
Thinline Telecaster '69 (J)	1986–onward
Thinline Telecaster '72 (J)	1986–onward
Limited Edition Jazz Bass '62	1987–89
Limited Edition Precision Bass '57	1987–89
Limited Edition Precision Bass '62	1987–89
Strat Plus	1987–98
American Standard Jazz Bass (1st version)	1988–94
American Standard Precision Bass (1st version)	1988–95
American Standard Telecaster	1988–2000
Blue Flower Stratocaster (1st version) (J)	1988–93
Eric Clapton Stratocaster (1st version)	1988–2001
HM Power Strat (2 variations) (J)	1988–89
Paisley Stratocaster (J)	1988–onward
Power Jazz Bass Special (J)	1988–91
Standard Jazz Bass (J)	1988–91
Standard Precision Bass Short-Scale (J)	1988–91
Standard Stratocaster (2nd version) (J)	1988–91
Standard Telecaster (J)	1988–91
Strat XII (J)	1988–onward
Yngwie Malmsteen Stratocaster (1st version)	1988–98
Stratocaster '68 (J)	1988–onward
American Standard Deluxe Stratocaster	1989–90
HM Strat (3 variations)	1989–90
Precision Bass Lyte (J)	1989–95
Precision Bass Plus	1989–92
Robben Ford (J)	1989–94
Short-Scale Precision Bass (J)	1989–91
Short-Scale Stratocaster (J)	1989–95
Strat Plus Deluxe	1989–98
US Contemporary Stratocaster	1989–91
50s Precision Bass (J)	1989–94
60s Jazz Bass (J)	1989–94
60s Precision Bass (J)	1989–94
Acoustic-Electric Precision Bass (J)	1990–94
Albert Collins Telecaster	1990–current
Danny Gatton Telecaster	1990–current
HM Bass	1990
HM Bass (J)	1990–92
HM Bass V	1990
HM Bass V (J)	1990–92
HM Bass Ultra	1990–92
HM Strat Ultra	1990–92
HRR Stratocaster (J)	1990–94
Jazz Plus Bass	1990–94
Jazz Plus V Bass	1990–94
JP-90 Bass	1990–94
James Burton Telecaster (1st version)	1990–2005
Strat Ultra	1990–98
Tele Plus (1st version)	1990–95
50s Telecaster (J)	1990–onward
HM Strat (2 variations) (J)	1991–92
HMT Acoustic-Electric (1st version) (J)	1991–94
HMT Acoustic-Electric Bass (J)	1991–92
HMT Telecaster (2 variations) (J)	1991–92
Jeff Beck Stratocaster (1st version)	1991–2001
Precision Bass Plus Deluxe	1991–94
Prodigy	1991–93
Prodigy Active Bass	1991–94
Prodigy II	1991–92
Robert Cray Stratocaster	1992–current
Set Neck Telecaster	1991–95
Set Neck Telecaster Floyd Rose	1991–92
Set Neck Telecaster Plus	1991–92
Standard Jazz Bass (M)	1991–current
Standard Precision Bass (M)	1991–current
Standard Stratocaster (M)	1991–current
Standard Telecaster (M)	1991–current
Tele Plus Deluxe	1991–92
Yngwie Malmsteen Standard Stratocaster (J)	1991–94
American Classic Stratocaster	1992–99
Bajo Sexto Telecaster baritone	1992–98
Floyd Rose Classic Stratocaster	1992–98
Floyd Rose HRR Stratocaster (J)	1992–94
JD Telecaster (J)	1992–99
Jerry Donahue Telecaster	1992–2001
Set Neck Stratocaster (1st version)	1992–95
Set Neck Floyd Rose Stratocaster	1992–95
Set Neck Telecaster Country Artist	1992–95
Sparkle Telecaster	1992–95
Squier Series Floyd Rose Standard Stratocaster (J)	1992–96
Squier Series Jazz Bass (K)	1992–94
Squier Series Precision Bass (K)	1992–94
Squier Series Stratocaster (K)	1992–94
Squier Series Telecaster (K)	1992–94
Stevie Ray Vaughan Stratocaster	1992–current
Stu Hamm Urge Bass	1992–99
Vintage Precision Custom Bass	1992–2000
'51 Precision Bass (J)	1992–98, 2003–current
'54 Stratocaster	1992–98
'60 Stratocaster (1st version)	1992–98
'75 Jazz Bass (J)	1992–99
50s Stratocaster Foto Flame (J)	1992–94
60s Stratocaster Foto Flame (J)	1992–94
70s Precision Bass (J)	1992–93
Clarence White Telecaster	1993–2001
DR-6 Bass (J)	1993
Duo-Sonic (M)	1993–97
Elan 1 (J)	1993
Prophecy PR-I Bass (J)	1993–94
Prophecy PR-II Bass (J)	1993–94
Prophecy PR-III Bass (J)	1993–94
Richie Sambora Stratocaster (1st version)	1993–99
RR-58 (J)	1993
Special Edition 1993 Stratocaster	1993
Stu Hamm Urge Standard Bass (M)	1993–99
Talon (J)	1993
Aluminum-Body Stratocaster (various models)	1994–95
Aluminum-Body Telecaster	1994–95
D'Aquisto Elite	1994–95, 2000–01
Dick Dale Stratocaster	1994–current
Floyd Rose Standard Stratocaster (M)	1994–98
Floyd Rose Standard Stratocaster (J)	1994–96

chronology 1950-2009

Jaguar Foto Flame (J)	1994–96
Jazzmaster Foto Flame (J)	1994–96
MB-4 Bass (J)	1994–96
MB-5 Bass (J)	1994–96
P-Bass Special (M)	1994–96
Richie Sambora Standard Stratocaster (M)	1994–2002
Robben Ford Elite	1994–2001
Robben Ford Ultra FM	1994–2001
Robben Ford Ultra SP	1994–2001
Special Edition 1994 Stratocaster	1994
Special Edition 1994 Telecaster	1994
Squier Series Floyd Rose Standard Stratocaster (M)	1994–96
Squier Series Standard Jazz Bass (M)	1994–96
Squier Series Standard Precision Bass (M)	1994–96
Squier Series Standard Stratocaster (M)	1994–96
Squier Series Standard Telecaster (M)	1994–96
Strat Special (M)	1994–96
Tele Special (M)	1994–96
50s Telecaster Foto Flame	1994
60s Jazz Bass Foto Flame (J)	1994–96
60s Precision Bass Foto Flame (J)	1994–96
60s Telecaster Foto Flame (J)	1994
40th Anniversary 1954 Stratocaster	1994
American Classic Telecaster (1st version)	1995–99
American Classic Jazz Bass	1995–96
American Classic Jazz FMT Bass	1995–96
American Classic Jazz V FMT Bass	1995–96
American Standard B-Bender Telecaster	1995–97
American Standard Jazz Bass (2nd version)	1995–2000
American Standard Jazz V Bass (1st version)	1995–2000
American Standard Precision Bass (2nd version)	1995–2000
American Standard Roland GR-Ready Stratocaster	1995–98
Bonnie Raitt Stratocaster	1995–2001
Buddy Guy Stratocaster	1995–current
Carved Top Strat	1995–98
Contemporary Strat	1995–98
Contemporary Strat FMT	1995–98
D'Aquisto Deluxe	1995–2001
Deluxe Jazz Bass	1995–98
Deluxe Jazz V Bass	1995–97
Deluxe Precision Bass	1995–98
Foto Flame Stratocaster (J)	1995–96
Foto Flame Telecaster (J)	1995–96
90s Telecaster Deluxe Foto Flame (J)	1995–96
HMT Acoustic-Electric (2nd version) (J)	1995–97
James Burton Standard Telecaster (M)	1995–current
Precision Bass Lyte Deluxe (J)	1995–2001
Precision Bass Lyte Standard (J)	1995–2001
Roscoe Beck Bass V	1995–2006
Set Neck Stratocaster (2nd version)	1995–98
Tele Jnr	1995–2000
Tele Plus (2nd version)	1995–98
Telecaster XII	1995–98

VI (aka "Bass VI") Reissue (J)	1995–98
Waylon Jennings Tribute Telecaster	1995–2003
'54 Stratocaster FMT	1995–98
'60 Stratocaster FMT	1995–98
90s Telecaster Custom (J)	1995–98
90s Telecaster Deluxe (J)	1995–98
Hank Marvin Stratocaster (J)	1996–97
Jag-Stang (J)	1996–onward
Lone Star Strat	1996–2000
Nokie Edwards Telecaster (J)	1996
Relic 50s Nocaster	1996–98
Relic 50s Stratocaster	1996–98
Relic 60s Jazz Bass	1996–98
Relic 60s Stratocaster	1996–98
Richie Sambora Paisley Stratocaster (J)	1996
Tex-Mex Strat (M)	1996–97
The Ventures Jazz Bass (J)	1996
The Ventures Jazzmaster (J)	1996
The Ventures Stratocaster (J)	1996
Traditional Jazz Bass (M)	1996–97
Traditional Precision Bass (M)	1996–97
Traditional Fat Strat (M)	1996–98
Traditional Stratocaster (M)	1996–98
Traditional Telecaster (M)	1996–98
'58 Stratocaster	1996–98
'69 Stratocaster (1st version)	1996–98
50s Telecaster	1996–98
60s Telecaster Custom	1996–98
50th Anniversary Jazz Bass	1996
50th Anniversary Precision Bass	1996
50th Anniversary Stratocaster	1996
50th Anniversary Telecaster	1996
Big Apple Strat	1997–2000
California Fat Strat	1997–98
California Fat Tele	1997–98
California Precision Bass Special	1997–98
California Strat	1997–98
California Tele	1997–98
Collectors Edition Stratocaster	1997
Deluxe Active Jazz Bass (M)	1997–current
Deluxe Nashville Tele (M)	1997–current
Deluxe Powerhouse Strat (M)	1997–current
Deluxe Super Strat (M)	1997–2004
Hank Marvin Stratocaster (M)	1997
Jerry Donahue Hellecasters Stratocaster (J)	1997–98
Jimi Hendrix Stratocaster	1997–2000
Jimmie Vaughan Tex-Mex Stratocaster (M)	1997–current
John Jorgenson Hellecaster (J)	1997–98
Merle Haggard Tele	1997–current
Noel Redding Jazz Bass (J)	1997
Ritchie Blackmore Stratocaster (J)	1997–98
Roadhouse Strat	1997–2000
Tex-Mex Strat Special (M)	1997
Tex-Mex Tele Special (M)	1997
Will Ray Jazz-A-Caster (J)	1997–98
90s Tele Thinline	1997–2001

American Deluxe Fat Strat	1998–2003
American Deluxe Fat Strat/Locking Trem	1998–2003
American Deluxe Jazz Bass	1998–current
American Deluxe Jazz Bass V	1998–current
American Deluxe Precision Bass	1998–current
American Deluxe Stratocaster (1st version)	1998–2003
American Deluxe Telecaster (1st version)	1998–99
American Standard Stratocaster Hard-Tail	1998–2000
American Vintage '62 Jazz Bass	1998–current
American Vintage '57 Precision Bass	1998–current
American Vintage '62 Precision Bass	1998–current
American Vintage '52 Telecaster	1998–current
American Vintage '57 Stratocaster	1998–current
American Vintage '62 Stratocaster	1998–current
Big Apple Strat Hard-Tail	1998–2000
Buck Owens Telecaster (J)	1998
Carved Top Strat HH	1998
Carved Top Strat HSS	1998
Classic Player Strat	1998–2005
Classic '69 Telecaster Thinline (M)	1998–current
Cyclone (M)	1998–2006
Deluxe Active Jazz V Bass (M)	1998–current
Deluxe Double Fat Strat Floyd Rose (M)	1998–2004
Deluxe Fat Strat Floyd Rose (M)	1998–2005
Donald "Duck" Dunn Precision Bass (J)	1998
Floyd Rose Classic Strat HH	1998–2002
Floyd Rose Classic Strat HSS	1998–2002
Geddy Lee Jazz Bass (J)	1998–current
John Jorgenson Telecaster	1998–2001
Marcus Miller Jazz Bass (J)	1998–current
Matthias Jabs Stratocaster (J)	1998
Nashville B-Bender Tele	1998–current
N.O.S. ('65) Strat	1998
Relic Floyd Rose Stratocaster	1998
Showmaster FMT	1998–2005
Standard Jazz Bass V (M)	1998–2008
Standard Roland Ready Strat (M)	1998–current
Tele-Sonic	1998–2004
Toronado (M)	1998–2004
U.S. Fat Tele / American Fat Tele	1998–2000, 01–03
Voodoo Stratocaster	1998–2000
Will Ray Telecaster	1998–2001
Yngwie Malmsteen Stratocaster (2nd version)	1998–2006
1998 Collectors Edition Telecaster	1998
American Classic Telecaster (2nd version)	1999–2000
American Deluxe Precision V Bass	1999–2006
American Deluxe Telecaster (2nd version)	1999–2003
American Deluxe Power Tele	1999–2001
American Vintage '52 Tele Special	1999–2001
American Vintage '62 Custom Telecaster	1999–current
American Vintage '62 Jaguar	1999–current
American Vintage '62 Jazzmaster	1999–current
American Vintage '75 Jazz Bass	1999–current
Chris Rea Classic Stratocaster (M)	1999
Classic 50s Stratocaster (M)	1999–current
Classic 50s Telecaster (M)	1999–current
Classic 60s Stratocaster (M)	1999–current

Classic 70s Stratocaster (M)	1999–current
Classic '72 Telecaster Custom (M)	1999–current
Classic '72 Telecaster Thinline (M)	1999–current
Custom Classic Strat	1999–2008
Deluxe Double Fat Strat (M)	1999–2004
Deluxe Fat Strat (M)	1999–current
Deluxe Nashville Power Tele (M)	1999–current
Deluxe Precision Bass Special (M)	1999–2004
Hot Rod Precision Bass	1999–2000
Jaco Pastorius Jazz Bass	1999–current
Jaco Pastorius Tribute Jazz Bass	1999–current
Richie Sambora Stratocaster (2nd version)	1999–2002
Ritchie Blackmore Stratocaster	1999–2005
Rocco Prestia Precision Bass	1999
Showmaster Set Neck FMT	1999–2005
Showmaster Set Neck FMT Hard-Tail	1999–2005
Showmaster Standard	1999–2005
Standard Fat Strat (M)	1999–2007
Standard Fat Strat Floyd Rose (M)	1999–2007
Stu Hamm Urge Bass II	1999–current
'51 Nocaster (Closet Classic/N.O.S./Relic)	1999–current
'56 Stratocaster (Closet Classic/N.O.S./Relic)	1999–current
'60 Stratocaster (2nd version) (Closet Classic/N.O.S./Relic)	1999–current
'63 Telecaster (Closet Classic/N.O.S./Relic)	1999–current
'64 Jazz Bass (Closet Classic/N.O.S./Relic)	1999–current
'69 Stratocaster (2nd version) (Closet Classic/N.O.S./Relic)	1999–current
American Jazz Bass	2000–07
American Jazz V Bass	2000–07
American Precision Bass	2000–07
American Stratocaster	2000–07
American Stratocaster Hard-Tail	2000–06
American Double Fat Strat	2000–03
American Double Fat Strat Hard-Tail	2000–03
American Fat Strat Texas Special	2000–03
American Strat Texas Special	2000–03
American Telecaster	2000–07
Classic Rocker	2000–02
Custom Classic Telecaster	2000–08
Hank Marvin Classic Stratocaster (M)	2000
Hot Rodded American Precision Bass	2000–07
Leo Fender Broadcaster	2000
Muddy Waters Tribute Telecaster	2000
Showmaster 7–string	2000–01
Showmaster 7–string Hard-Tail	2000–01
Sub-Sonic Stratocaster HH baritone	2000–01
Sub-Sonic Stratocaster HSS baritone (1st version)	2000–01
'59 Precision Bass (Closet Classic/N.O.S./Relic)	2000–08
American Deluxe Jazz Bass FMT/QMT	2001–06
American Deluxe Zone Bass	2001–06
American Fat Tele	2001–03
Classic 60s Telecaster (M)	2001–current
Custom Classic Jazz Bass	2001–08
Custom Classic Jazz Bass V	2001–08

Deluxe Zone Bass (M)	2001–06
Eric Clapton Stratocaster (2nd version)	2001–04
Iron Maiden Signature Stratocaster (J)	2001–02
Jeff Beck Stratocaster (2nd version)	2001–04
Muddy Waters Telecaster (M)	2001–current
Steve Harris Signature Precision Bass (J)	2001, 2009–current
Sting Signature Precision Bass (J)	2001–current
Sub-Sonic Stratocaster HSS baritone (2nd version)	2001
Sub-Sonic Tele baritone	2001–05
Tom Delonge Stratocaster (M)	2001–03
Victor Bailey Jazz Bass	2001–current
1951 Anniversary Precision Bass	2001
50th Anniversary American Precision Bass	2001
American Deluxe Jazz Bass V FMT/QMT	2002–06
Buddy Guy Polka Dot/Standard Strat (M)	2002–current
Classic Mustang Bass (J)	2002–current
Competition Mustang (J)	2002–03
Cyclone II (M)	2002–06
Deluxe Double Fat Strat HH (M)	2002–03
Deluxe Double Fat Strat HH With Locking Tremolo (M)	2002–03
Deluxe Fat Strat HSS (M)	2002–03
Deluxe Fat Strat HSS With Locking Tremolo (M)	2002–03
Highway One Stratocaster (1st version)	2002–06
Highway One Telecaster (1st version)	2002–06
Mark Hoppus Precision Bass (M)	2002–current
Reggie Hamilton Jazz Bass	2002–current
Reggie Hamilton Jazz Bass V	2002–current
Standard Fat Strat With Locking Tremolo (M)	2002–03
Strat Special With Locking Tremolo HH	2002
Strat Special With Locking Tremolo HSS	2002
Toronado DVII	2002–04
Toronado HH	2002–04
'68 Reverse Strat Special	2002
Aerodyne Jazz Bass (J)	2003–current
American Ash Telecaster	2003–current
American Stratocaster HH	2003–06
American Stratocaster HH Hard-Tail	2003–05
American Stratocaster HSS	2003–07
American Telecaster HH (1st version)	2003–04
American Telecaster HS (1st version)	2003–04
Blue Flower Stratocaster (2nd version) (J)	2003
Custom Telecaster FMT HH (K)	2003–current
Cyclone HH (M)	2003–05
Esquire Custom Celtic (K)	2003
Esquire Custom GT (K)	2003
Esquire Custom Scorpion (K)	2003
Flat Head Showmaster	2003–04
Flat Head Telecaster	2003–04
Francis Rossi Signature Telecaster (J)	2003–04
Highway One Jazz Bass (1st version)	2003–06
Highway One Precision Bass (1st version)	2003–06
Highway One Showmaster HH	2003–04
Highway One Showmaster HSS	2003–04
Highway One Stratocaster HSS (1st version)	2003–06
Highway One Texas Telecaster	2003–current
Highway One Toronado	2003–04
J5:Bigsby	2003–current

J5:HB Telecaster	2003–current
Jimmy Bryant Telecaster	2003–05
Marcus Miller Jazz Bass V	2003–current
Mark Knopfler Stratocaster	2003–current
Rick Parfitt Signature Telecaster (J)	2003–04
Robert Cray Stratocaster (M)	2003–current
Showmaster Celtic H (K)	2003
Showmaster Deluxe HH With Tremolo (K)	2003
Showmaster H With Tremolo (K)	2003
Showmaster HH With Tremolo (K)	2003
Showmaster Scorpion HH (K)	2003
Seymour Duncan Signature Esquire	2003–current
Splatter Stratocaster (M)	2003
Standard Satin Stratocaster (M)	2003–06
Strat-O-Sonic DVI	2003–04
Strat-O-Sonic DVII	2003–06
'54 Blue Flower Precision (J)	2003
'54 Paisley Precision (J)	2003
'55 Precision Bass	2003–06
'59 Esquire	2003–06
'60 Telecaster Custom (Closet Classic/N.O.S./Relic)	2003–04
'65 Stratocaster (Closet Classic/N.O.S./Relic)	2003–06
Aerodyne Stratocaster (1st version) (J)	2004
Aerodyne Tele (J)	2004–06
American Deluxe Ash Jazz Bass	2004–current
American Deluxe Ash Jazz Bass V	2004–current
American Deluxe Ash Precision Bass	2004–06
American Deluxe Ash Precision Bass V	2004–06
American Deluxe Ash Stratocaster	2004–current
American Deluxe Ash Telecaster	2004–current
American Deluxe Stratocaster (2nd version)	2004–current
American Deluxe Stratocaster FMT HSS	2004–current
American Deluxe Stratocaster HSS	2004–current
American Deluxe Stratocaster HSS LT	2004–06
American Deluxe Stratocaster QMT HSS	2004–current
American Deluxe Stratocaster V Neck	2004–current
American Deluxe Telecaster (3rd version)	2004–current
American Deluxe Telecaster FMT	2004–06
American Deluxe Telecaster QMT	2004–06
American Deluxe 50th Anniversary Stratocaster	2004
American Telecaster HH (2nd version)	2004–06
American Telecaster HS (2nd version)	2004–06
American 50th Anniversary Stratocaster	2004
Antigua Jaguar (J)	2004
Antigua Stratocaster (J)	2004
Antigua Telecaster (J)	2004
Blackout Telecaster HH (K)	2004
Classic '72 Telecaster Deluxe (M)	2004–current
Classic 60s Jazz Bass (M)	2004–current
Deluxe Player's Strat (M)	2004–current
Deluxe Strat HH (M)	2004
Deluxe Strat HH With Locking Tremolo (M)	2004
Deluxe Strat HSS (M)	2004–06
Deluxe Strat HSS With Locking Tremolo (M)	2004–05
Dimension Bass (M)	2004–06
Eric Clapton Stratocaster (3rd version)	2004–current
Flat Head Showmaster HH	2004–06
Flat Head Telecaster HH	2004–06
Jaguar Baritone Custom (J)	2004–06
Jeff Beck Signature Stratocaster	2004–current

chronology 1950-2009

John 5 Telecaster (M)	2004–current	
Lite Ash Stratocaster (K)	2004–08	
Lite Ash Telecaster (K)	2004–08	
Mark Dirnt Precision Bass (M)	2004–current	
Rory Gallagher Stratocaster	2004–current	
Roscoe Beck Bass IV	2004–current	
Showmaster Blackout (K)	2004–05	
Showmaster Elite FMT/LWT/QMT/SMT	2004–08	
Showmaster Elite Hard-Tail	2004–07	
Showmaster Fat-HH (K)	2004–05	
Showmaster Fat-SSS (K)	2004–05	
Showmaster QBT-HH (K)	2004–07	
Showmaster QBT-SSS (K)	2004–05	
Standard Stratocaster HH (M)	2004–06	
Standard Stratocaster HSS (M)	2004–current	
Standard Stratocaster HSS With Locking Tremolo/Floyd Rose (M)	2004–current	
Stevie Ray Vaughan Tribute Stratocaster	2004	
TC-90 Thinline (K)	2004–07	
'66 Stratocaster (Closet Classic/N.O.S./Relic)	2004–08	
50th Anniversary 1954 Stratocaster	2004	
50th Anniversary Golden Stratocaster (M)	2004	
Aerodyne Stratocaster (2nd version) (J)	2005–06	
Classic 50s Esquire (M)	2005–current	
Classic 50s Precision Bass (M)	2005–current	
Deluxe Active Precision Bass Special (M)	2005–current	
Deluxe Big Block Precision Bass (M)	2005–08	
Deluxe Big Block Stratocaster (M)	2005–06	
Deluxe Big Block Telecaster (M)	2005–06	
Eric Johnson Stratocaster	2005–current	
Jaguar Baritone HH (J)	2005–current	
Jaguar HH (J)	2005–current	
Jazz Bass 24 (K)	2005–current	
John Mayer Stratocaster	2005–current	
Mary Kaye Tribute Stratocaster	2005	
Reggie Hamilton Standard Jazz Bass (M)	2005–current	
Richie Kotzen Signature Telecaster (J)	2005–06	
Robin Trower Stratocaster	2005–current	
Showmaster FMT-HH (K)	2005–current	
Showmaster QMT-HH (K)	2005–current	
So-Cal Speed Shop (K)	2005	
Standard Stratocaster FMT (M)	2005–06	
Strat-O-Sonic HH	2005–06	
Tie-Dye Strat HS (K)	2005	
Toronado GT HH (K)	2005–06	
Toronado HH (M)	2005–06	
'67 Telecaster (Closet Classic/N.O.S./Relic)	2005–08	
50s Telecaster With Bigsby (J)	2005–06	
60s Telecaster With Bigsby (J)	2005–current	
Aerodyne Classic Precision Bass Special (J)	2006–08	
Aerodyne Classic Stratocaster (J)	2006–current	
American Vintage 70s Stratocaster	2006–current	
American 60th Anniversary Stratocaster	2006	
American 60th Anniversary Telecaster	2006	
American 60th Anniversary Jazz Bass	2006	
American 60th Anniversary Precision Bass	2006	

Classic Player Baja Telecaster (M)	2006–current	
Classic Player 50s Stratocaster (M)	2006–current	
Classic Player 60s Stratocaster (M)	2006–current	
Deluxe Power Jazz Bass (M)	2006–08	
Deluxe Power Stratocaster (M)	2006–current	
Eric Clapton Tribute Blackie Stratocaster	2006	
Highway One Jazz Bass (2nd version)	2006–current	
Highway One Precision Bass (2nd version)	2006–current	
Highway One Stratocaster (2nd version)	2006–current	
Highway One Stratocaster HSS (2nd version)	2006–current	
Highway One Telecaster (2nd version)	2006–current	
Jaguar Bass (J)	2006–current	
Jaguar Bass VI Custom (J)	2006	
James Burton Telecaster (2nd version)	2006–current	
Koa Stratocaster (K)	2006–08	
Koa Telecaster (K)	2006–08	
Pino Palladino Precision Bass	2006–current	
Standard 60th Anniversary Precision Bass (M)	2006	
Standard 60th Anniversary Stratocaster (M)	2006	
Strat Pro	2006–current	
Tele Thinline	2006–current	
Tony Franklin Fretless Precision Bass	2006–current	
Victor Bailey Jazz Bass V	2006–current	
'65 Mustang Reissue (J)	2006–current	
American VG Stratocaster	2007–09	
American Vintage 1957 Commemorative Stratocaster	2007	
Duff McKagan Bass (M)	2007–current	
Eric Clapton Crossroads Stratocaster	2007	
G.E. Smith Telecaster	2007–current	
George Fullerton 50th Anniversary Stratocaster	2007	
J. Mascis Jazzmaster (J)	2007–current	
Jazz Bass 24 V (K)	2007–current	
Joe Strummer Tele (M)	2007–current	
Joe Strummer Tribute Telecaster	2007	
J5 Triple Tele Deluxe (M)	2007–current	
Stevie Ray Vaughan Tribute Lenny Stratocaster	2007	
Tele Pro	2007–current	
Tony Franklin Fretted Precision Bass	2007–current	
Vintage Hot Rod '52 Tele	2007–current	
Vintage Hot Rod '57 Strat	2007–current	
Vintage Hot Rod '62 Strat	2007–current	
Yngwie Malmsteen Stratocaster (3rd version)	2007–current	
American Nashville B-Bender Telecaster	2008–current	
American Standard Jazz Bass (3rd version)	2008–current	
American Standard Jazz Bass V (2nd version)	2008–current	
American Standard Precision Bass (3rd version)	2008–current	
American Standard Precision Bass V	2008–current	
American Standard Stratocaster (2nd version)	2008–current	
American Standard Stratocaster HSS	2008–current	

American Standard Stratocaster Roland Ready	2008–current	
American Standard Telecaster (2nd version)	2008–current	
Billy Corgan Stratocaster	2008–current	
Classic Player Jaguar (M)	2008–current	
Classic Player Jaguar HH (M)	2008–current	
Classic Player Jazzmaster (M)	2008–current	
Classic 60s Telecaster W/Bigsby (M)	2008–current	
Classic 70s Jazz Bass (M)	2008–current	
David Gilmour Stratocaster	2008–current	
Deluxe Acoustasonic Strat (M)	2008–current	
Deluxe Blackout Tele (M)	2008–current	
Deluxe Lone Star Stratocaster (M)	2008–current	
Deluxe Roadhouse Stratocaster (M)	2008–current	
Elvis Costello Jazzmaster	2008–current	
Frank Bello Bass (M)	2008–current	
Jazzmaster-Coustic	2008	
Jim Root Telecaster (M)	2008–current	
Spalted Maple Tele (J)	2008–current	
Victor Bailey Jazz Bass Fretless	2008–current	
'64 Bass VI	2008	
Classic HBS-1 Stratocaster (N.O.S./Relic)	2009–current	
Classic S-1 Telecaster (N.O.S./Relic)	2009–current	
Custom Deluxe Stratocaster	2009–current	
Custom Deluxe Telecaster	2009–current	
Dave Murray Stratocaster	2009–current	
JA-90 Telecaster (K)	2009–current	
Kenny Wayne Shepherd Stratocaster (M)	2009–current	
Lee Ranaldo Jazzmaster	2009–current	
Ritchie Blackmore Stratocaster (M)	2009–current	
Road Worn 50s Precision Bass (M)	2009–current	
Road Worn 50s Stratocaster (M)	2009–current	
Road Worn 60s Jazz Bass (M)	2009–current	
Road Worn 60s Stratocaster (M)	2009–current	
Road Worn 50s Telecaster (M)	2009–current	
Steve Bailey Jazz Bass VI	2009–current	
Thurston Moore Jazzmaster	2009–current	
'64 Stratocaster Relic	2009	
'64 Telecaster Relic	2009	
50s Telecaster Thinline (N.O.S./Relic)	2009	

index

index

acknowledgements

INSTRUMENT OWNERS
The guitars we photographed came from the collections of the following individuals and organizations, and we're grateful for their help. They are listed here in the alphabetical order of the code used to identify their instruments in the Key below. **AB** Andrew Bodnar; **AG** Arbiter Group; **AH** Adrian Hornbrook; **AK** Alan Hardtke; **AR** Alan Rogan; **BC** The Bass Centre; **BD** Bob Daisley; **BM** Barry Moorhouse; **BW** Bruce Welch; **CC** The Chinery Collection; **CN** Carl Nielsen; **DG** David Gilmour; **DM** Dixie's Music; **FJ** Fender Japan; **FM** Fender Musical Instruments Corporation; **GG** Gruhn Guitars; **GH** George Harrison; **GM** Graeme Matheson; **JE** John Entwistle; **MB** Mandolin Brothers; **MG** Music Ground; **MM** Marcus Miller; **MP** Martin Petersen; **PD** Paul Day; **PM** Paul Midgley; **RB** Robin Baird; **RG** Robin Guthrie; **RY** Rory Gallagher; **RT** Randy Hope-Taylor; **SA** Scot Arch; **SB** Sam Benjamin; **SC** Simon Carlton; **SH** Steve Howe; **SL** Steve Lewis; **TB** Tony Bacon; **TP** Tim Philips.

KEY TO INSTRUMENT PHOTOGRAPHS
The following key is designed to identify who owned which guitars at the time they were photographed. After the relevant bold-type page number(s) we list the model name followed by the owner's initials (see Instrument Owners above). **7**: Broadcaster DG. **8**: Telecaster GG; Esquire DG. **9**: Precision JE. **11**: Student SH; Deluxe AR. **13**: Stringmaster SH. **15**: 0001 Strat DG; sunburst Strat SC. **17**: Champ SH; Tremolux AK. **19**: Duo-Sonic RG; Musicmaster RG. **21**: Precision BD; Strat MB. **23**: Jazzmaster CC. **25**: Tele Custom AH; Strat BW. **29**: Jazz Bass JE. **31**: VI JE; Showman AR. **33**: Jaguar RG. **35**: Palomino AB; Twin AR. **37**: Mustang RB; Strat SA; Jazzmaster CC. **38**: Bass V BC. **39**: Electric XII RB; Marauder GG. **41**: Coronado GM; Mustang Bass BC. **43**: Bronco RB; Strat GH. **45**: Tele AH; Montego RB; LTD RB. **47**: Custom RB; Swinger PD. **51**: Precision BC; Tele AH. **53**: Tele humbuckers CN; Tele regular PM. **55**: Tele Bass humbucker TB; ele Bass single-coil RG; Strat RY. **57**: Tele PM. **59**: Jazz Bass MG. **61**: Strat PD. **63**: Starcaster TP. **65**: Mustang Bass BC; Strat PM. **69**: Strat SC. **73**: Strat PM. **75**: Bullet DM; Strat taupe PD; Strat orange SC. **77**: Jazz Bass RT; Strat BM. **79**: Tele PD; '57 Strat DG; Standard Strat SL. **81**: D'Aquisto PD. **83**: Performer PM; Katana PD. **85**: Strat PM. **87**: Strat PM. **89**: Clapton Strat PM; Strat XII PM; Blue Flower Strat FJ. **91**: double-neck FM; Heartfield FM. **95**: Tele PM; Jazz Plus V SB. **97**: Prodigy FM; Tele FM; Precision MP. **99**: Strat FM; Urge Bass AG. **100**: Strat FM; Tele FM. **103**: Strat FM; Robben Ford FM. **105**: both Strats FM. **106**: Jag-Stang AG; Strat AG. **108**: Venus AG. **109**: two Strats AG; Super-Sonic AG. **110**: Cyclone AG. **111**: Toronado AG; Jazz Bass MM. **113**: Jazz Bass BC. **116**: Leo Broadcaster AG; Classic Rocker FM. **119** Strat FM; Precision FM. **121** Tele FM; Starfire FM. **122** Tele FM. **123** HSS Strat FM; Knopfler Strat FM; Tele FM. **125** Showmaster FM; Tele FM; Strat FM. **126** Jazz 24 FM. **127** Tele FM; M-80 FM; Strat FM. **129** Blackie FM; Kitty FM; Strat FM. **130** Strat FM. **131** Jazzmaster FM; Tele FM. **132** Strat FM; Jazzmaster-Coustic FM. **133** Jazzmaster FM. **135** Jazz Bass FM; Strat FM.

Principal guitar photography is by Miki Slingsby. A few guitar pictures were taken by Garth Blore and Matthew Chattle.

ARTIST PICTURES are identified by bold-type page number, subject, and photographer or collection and agency (R = Redferns). *8–9* Holly, Michael Ochs Archive/Getty Images. *21* Dunn, Michael Ochs Archive/Getty Images. *26–27* Hendrix, David Redfern/R. *32* Cropper, Michael Ochs Archive/Getty Images. *33* Beach Boys, Michael Ochs Archive/Getty Images. *43* Harrison, Susie MacDonald/R. *46* Hendrix, David Redfern/R. *48–49* Clapton, David Redfern/R. *57* George, Ian Dickson/R. *58* Graham, Gems/Redferns. *61* Wailers, Ian Dickson/R. *66* Knopfler, Mike Prior/R; Rodgers, Ebet Roberts/R; Talking Heads, Ebet Roberts/R. *67* Costello, Keith Morris/R; Police, Ebet Roberts/R. *69* Cure, Bob King/R. *70–71* Edge, Ebet Roberts/R. *73* Iron Maiden, Susie MacDonald/R. *80* Los Lobos, Brigitte Engl/R. *81* Marr, Donna Santisi/R. *82* Edge, Ebet Roberts/R. *83* Collins, Finn Costello/R. *86* Moore, John Lynn Kirk/R. *92–93* Cobain, Ebet Roberts/R. *97* Mascis, Ebet Roberts/R. *99* Frusciante, Ebet Roberts/R. *101* Phair, Ann Stern/R. *103* Coxon, Henrietta Butler/R. *105* Guy, David Redfern/R. *106* Cobain, Ebet Roberts/R. *108* Love, Mick Hutson/R. *116* Coldplay, Nigel Crane/R. *117* Yorke, Patrick Ford/R. *118* Adams, Paul Bergen/R. *120* Nicholls, Martin Philbey/R. *124* Gilmour, Jim Steele/R. *125* Dirnt, Peter Still/R. *126* Walla, Christina Radish/R. *129* Arctic Monkeys, Tabatha Fireman/R. *130* Greenwood, Peter Pakvis/R. *133* Schmidt, Rob Verhorst/R. *134* Neil, Neil Lupin/R.

MEMORABILIA illustrated in the book including advertisements, brochures, catalogs, color charts, magazines, schematics, photographs, record jackets, and tags (in fact anything that isn't a guitar) came from the collections of Scot Arch, Tony Bacon, Balafon Image Bank, Paul Day, Fender Musical Instruments Corporation, Dave Gregory, George Martin, *The Music Trades*, The National Jazz Archive (Loughton), John Page, Ian Purser, Don Randall, Alan Rogan, and Steve Soest (Soest Guitar Repair).

THANKS to the following people for help with this book (and the earlier book upon which this one is based, *50 Years Of Fender*), in addition to those already named above: Julie Bowie; Paul Day; Mike Eldred (Fender Musical Instruments Corporation); Jason Farrell (FMIC); Clay Harrell; Jake Hill (FMIC); Danny Jones (Arbiter Group); Dixie Kidd (Dixie's Music); Mike Lewis (FMIC); Barry Moorhouse (Bass Centre); Jun Nakabayashi (Fender Japan); Shane Nicholas (FMIC); Justin Norvell (FMIC); Nick Owen (Bass Centre); John Page (p-one-c.com); John Reynolds (Golden Age Guitars); Julian Ridgway (Redferns); Alan Rogan; Richard Siegle (FMIC); Dan Smith (FMIC); Sally Stockwell; Neil Whitcher (Fender GB & Ireland).

BOOKS
Tony Bacon *A Complete History Of Fender Instruments* (Backbeat 2007); *50 Years Of Fender* (Backbeat 2000); *The Fender Electric Guitar Book* (Backbeat 2007); *The History Of The American Guitar* (Balafon/Friedman Fairfax 2001); *Six Decades Of The Fender Telecaster* (Backbeat 2005).
Tony Bacon (ed) *Echo & Twang* (Backbeat 2001); *Electric Guitars: The Illustrated Encyclopedia* (Thunder Bay 2009); *Feedback & Fuzz* (Miller Freeman 2000); *2,000 Guitars* (Thunder Bay 2009).
Tony Bacon & Barry Moorhouse *The Bass Book* (Backbeat 2008).
Tony Bacon & Paul Day *The Ultimate Guitar Book* (DK/Knopf 1991).
Bill Carson *My Life And Times With Fender Musical Instruments* (Hal Leonard 1999).
Walter Carter & George Gruhn *Gruhn's Guide To Vintage Guitars* (Miller Freeman 1999).
Scott Chinery & Tony Bacon *The Chinery Collection – 150 Years Of American Guitars* (Balafon 1996).
Alan di Perna *Fender Classic Moments* (Hal Leonard 1995).
A.R. Duchossoir *The Fender Stratocaster* (Mediapresse 1988); *The Fender Telecaster* (Hal Leonard 1991); *Guitar Identification* (Hal Leonard 1990).
Fender *Custom Shop Guitar Gallery* (Fender/Hal Leonard 1996).
George Fullerton *Guitar Legends: The Evolution Of The Guitar From Fender to G&L* (Centerstream 1993).
Guitar Magazine (Japan) *The Fender 1: Stratocaster* (Rittor 1987); *The Fender 2: Telecaster & Other Guitars* (Rittor 1993).
Steve Howe & Tony Bacon *The Steve Howe Guitar Collection* (Balafon 1994).
Ray Minhinnett & Bob Young *The Story Of The Fender Stratocaster* (IMP 1995).
John Morrish *The Fender Amp Book* (Balafon/Miller Freeman 1995).

Richard R. Smith *Fender: The Sound Heard 'Round The World* (Garfish 1995).
John Teagle & John Sprung *Fender Amps: The First Fifty Years* (Fender/Hal Leonard 1995).
Tom Wheeler *American Guitars* (HarperPerennial 1990); *The Soul Of Tone: Celebrating 60 Years Of Fender Amps* (Hal Leonard 2007); *The Stratocaster Chronicles* (Hal Leonard 2004).
Forrest White *Fender: The Inside Story* (Miller Freeman 1994).
YMM Player *We Love Fender Guitars* (Player Corporation 1982); *History Of Electric Guitars* (Player Corporation 1988).

BACK ISSUES We consulted old copies of the following magazines: *Bass Player, Beat Instrumental, Down Beat, Fender Bridge, Fender Facts, Fender Frontline, Guitar (Japan), Guitar & Bass, Guitar Player, Guitar World, Melody Maker, Metronome, Music Business, Music Industry, The Music Trades, Vintage Guitar, 20th Century Guitar.*

UPDATES? The author and publisher welcome any new information for future editions. You can email us at fendersixty@jawbonepress.com or you can write to Fender 60, Backbeat UK, 2A Union Court, 20-22 Union Road, London SW4 6JP, England.

"I didn't really think about revolutionizing the industry or anything of that sort. We were spending all of our time thinking about doing a better job for the musician."
Leo Fender